Stimmt!

Edexcel GCSE (9–1) German
Higher
Vocabulary Book

Pearson

Published by Pearson Education Limited, 80 Strand, London, WC2R 0RL
www.pearsonschoolsandfecolleges.co.uk
Text © Pearson Education Limited 2017
Editorial management by Gwladys Rushworth for Haremi
Edited by Anne Urbschat
Typeset by York Publishing Solutions Pvt. Ltd.
Cover image: Shutterstock.com: Bildagentur Zoonar GmbH
Cover © Pearson Education Limited 2017

Written by Melissa Weir

First published 2017
10

British Library Cataloguing in Publication Data
A catalogue record for this book is available from the British Library.
ISBN 978 1 292 13241 9

Copyright notice
All rights reserved. No part of this publication may be reproduced in any form or by any means (including photocopying or storing it in any medium by electronic means and whether or not transiently or incidentally to some other use of this publication) without the written permission of the copyright owner, except in accordance with the provisions of the Copyright, Design and Patents Act 1988 or under the terms of a license issued by the Copyright Licensing Agency, Barnard's Inn, 86 Fetter Lane, London EC4A 1EN (www.cla.co.uk). Applications for the copyright owner's written permission should be addressed to the publisher.

Printed in the UK by Ashford Colour Press

Inhalt

High-frequency words **4**

Kapitel 1
Words I should know for speaking and writing activities **13**
Extra words I should know for reading and listening activities **16**

Kapitel 2
Words I should know for speaking and writing activities **17**
Extra words I should know for reading and listening activities **20**

Kapitel 3
Words I should know for speaking and writing activities **21**
Extra words I should know for reading and listening activities **24**

Kapitel 4
Words I should know for speaking and writing activities **26**
Extra words I should know for reading and listening activities **29**

Kapitel 5
Words I should know for speaking and writing activities **30**
Extra words I should know for reading and listening activities **33**

Kapitel 6
Words I should know for speaking and writing activities **34**
Extra words I should know for reading and listening activities **37**

Kapitel 7
Words I should know for speaking and writing activities **38**
Extra words I should know for reading and listening activities **41**

Kapitel 8
Words I should know for speaking and writing activities **42**
Extra words I should know for reading and listening activities **45**

High-frequency words

Common verbs

abfahren	to depart
ankommen	to arrive
sich beeilen	to hurry
besuchen	to visit
bleiben	to stay
eintreten	to enter
fahren	to drive
fallen	to fall
hineingehen	to enter
sich hinsetzen	to sit down
kommen	to come
laufen	to walk, to run
einen Spaziergang machen	to go for a walk
spazieren	to walk
springen	to jump
steigen	to climb, to get on
verlassen	to leave (a place)
vorbeigehen	to pass by
zurückfahren	to return
zurückgehen	to return
zurückkehren	to return
zurückkommen	to come back

Had a look ☐ Nearly there ☐ Nailed it ☐

begleiten	to accompany
bringen	to bring, to take
fliehen	to escape
folgen	to follow
führen	to lead
landen	to land
fallen lassen	to drop
leben	to live (to be alive)
nehmen	to take
parken	to park
schlafen	to sleep
sterben	to die
stoppen	to stop
warten auf	to wait for
wohnen	to live (in a)
lassen	to leave
legen	to lay
liegen	to lie
sitzen	to sit
werfen	to throw

Had a look ☐ Nearly there ☐ Nailed it ☐

aufmachen	to open
sich befinden	to be located
begegnen	to meet
berühren	to touch
drücken	to push
halten	to stop, to hold
holen	to fetch
kleben	to stick, to glue
klopfen	to knock
laden	to load, to charge
öffnen	to open
schlagen	to knock, to hit
schließen	to shut
stecken	to put
stellen	to put
tragen	to wear, to carry
zumachen	to close, to shut
zurückstellen	to put back

Had a look ☐ Nearly there ☐ Nailed it ☐

sich amüsieren	to enjoy oneself
arbeiten	to work
ausleihen	to lend
einladen	to invite
einschlafen	to fall asleep
essen	to eat
fressen	to eat (animal)
fernsehen	to watch television
forschen	to research
klettern	to climb
sich kümmern um	to look after
sich langweilen	to be bored
lernen	to learn
lesen	to read
schenken	to give (presents)
studieren	to study (at university)
im Internet surfen	to surf the internet
(sich) treffen	to meet
trinken	to drink
verbringen	to spend (time)

Had a look ☐ Nearly there ☐ Nailed it ☐

sich ärgern	to be annoyed
bedauern	to regret
sich erinnern (an)	to remember
fühlen	to feel
gehören	to belong
helfen	to help
lächeln	to smile
lachen	to laugh
leid tun	to be sorry
lieben	to love
lügen	to tell a lie
meinen	to think, to say
(sich) streiten	to argue
vergeben	to forgive
vergessen	to forget
vermissen	to miss

4

High-frequency words

verpassen	to miss	anfangen	to begin
versprechen	to promise	aufhören	to stop
verzeihen	to forgive	beenden	to end
weinen	to cry	beginnen	to begin
wissen	to know	dauern	to last
wünschen	to wish	enden	to finish, to end
		erreichen	to reach

Had a look ☐ **Nearly there** ☐ **Nailed it** ☐

		geschehen	to happen
		gewinnen	to win
anrufen	to phone	nachsehen	to check
antworten	to answer	notieren	to note
beantworten	to answer	organisieren	to organise
beschreiben	to describe	passieren	to happen
besprechen	to discuss	planen	to plan
sich bewerben um	to apply for	produzieren	to produce
denken	to think	scheitern	to fail
diskutieren	to discuss	schiefgehen	to go wrong
erklären	to explain	verbessern	to improve
erzählen	to tell	verlieren	to lose
fragen	to ask	versuchen	to try
informieren	to inform	vorstellen	to introduce
mitteilen	to inform		

Had a look ☐ **Nearly there** ☐ **Nailed it** ☐

plaudern	to chat		
reden	to talk		
sagen	to say	bedienen	to serve
schreiben	to write	befehlen	to order (command)
sprechen	to speak	benutzen	to use
eine Frage stellen	to ask a question	beraten	to advise
telefonieren (mit)	to phone	bestellen	to order (food)
tippen	to type	bitten um	to ask for
unterschreiben	to sign	danken	to thank
wiederholen	to repeat	empfehlen	to recommend
zuhören	to listen	füllen	to fill

Had a look ☐ **Nearly there** ☐ **Nailed it** ☐

		geben	to give
		gelingen	to succeed
		raten	to advise
annehmen	to accept	reparieren	to repair
bekommen	to receive	reservieren	to reserve
beschließen	to decide	retten	to save, to rescue
bevorzugen	to prefer	schicken	to send
brauchen	to need	wechseln	to change
sich entscheiden	to decide		

Had a look ☐ **Nearly there** ☐ **Nailed it** ☐

erhalten	to receive		
erlauben	to allow		
erwarten	to expect	finden	to find
fehlen	to be missing	glauben	to believe, to think
sich freuen auf	to look forward to	haben	to have
gefallen	to please	heißen	to be called
gern haben	to like	hoffen	to hope
hassen	to hate	hören	to hear
sich interessieren für	to be interested in	kennen	to know (be familiar with)
verhindern	to prevent	nennen	to name
vermeiden	to avoid	schauen	to look
vorhaben	to intend	scheinen	to seem, to shine
werden	to become	sehen	to see

Had a look ☐ **Nearly there** ☐ **Nailed it** ☐

verstehen	to understand
wählen	to choose, to dial

High-frequency words

zeigen	*to show*
dürfen	*to be allowed to*
können	*to be able to*
mögen	*to like*
müssen	*to have to*
sollen	*to be supposed to*
wollen	*to want*
zusehen	*to look, to watch*

Had a look ☐ **Nearly there** ☐ **Nailed it** ☐

ausgeben	*to spend (money)*
einkaufen	*to shop*
einschalten	*to light, to turn on*
kaufen	*to buy*
klicken	*to click*
klingeln	*to ring*
kosten	*to cost*
leihen	*to borrow, to hire*
mieten	*to rent, to hire*
schneien	*to snow*
schweigen	*to be silent*
stehlen	*to steal*
verdienen	*to earn*
verkaufen	*to sell*
zahlen	*to pay*
zählen	*to count*

Had a look ☐ **Nearly there** ☐ **Nailed it** ☐

Common adjectives

ärgerlich	*annoying*
böse	*angry*
dumm	*stupid*
eilig	*in a hurry*
ermüdend	*tiring*
ernst	*serious*
erschöpft	*exhausted*
faul	*lazy*
launisch	*moody*
laut	*loud, noisy*
müde	*tired*
schüchtern	*shy*
schwach	*weak*
schwer	*heavy, serious*
streng	*strict*
traurig	*sad*
zornig	*angry*

Had a look ☐ **Nearly there** ☐ **Nailed it** ☐

artig	*well-behaved*
brav	*well-behaved*
beschäftigt	*busy*
dankbar	*grateful*
dynamisch	*dynamic*
fleißig	*hard-working*

geduldig	*patient*
gesund	*healthy*
glücklich	*happy*
gut gelaunt	*in a good mood*
komisch	*funny, comical*
lustig	*funny*
nett	*kind, nice*
reif	*mature, ripe*
reizend	*charming*
schnell	*fast, quick*
stark	*strong*
stolz	*proud*
verantwortlich	*responsible*
zufrieden	*satisfied*

Had a look ☐ **Nearly there** ☐ **Nailed it** ☐

groß	*big, tall*
klein	*little, small*
lang	*long*
kurz	*short*
hoch	*high*
niedrig	*low*
breit	*broad*
schmal	*slim, narrow*
dicht	*dense*
eng	*narrow, tight*
dünn	*thin*
rund	*round*
steil	*steep*
nah	*near*
weit	*far*
voll	*full*
leer	*empty*
erst–	*first*
letzt–	*last*
nächst–	*next*

Had a look ☐ **Nearly there** ☐ **Nailed it** ☐

alt	*old*
jung	*young*
jünger	*younger*
dick	*fat*
schlank	*slim*
hübsch	*pretty*
schön	*beautiful*
hässlich	*ugly*
krank	*ill*
reich	*rich*
satt	*full*

Had a look ☐ **Nearly there** ☐ **Nailed it** ☐

gut	*good*
ausgezeichnet	*excellent*
fantastisch	*fantastic*

High-frequency words

großartig	*magnificent*	unterschiedlich	*variable*
klasse	*sensational*	wertvoll	*valuable*
perfekt	*perfect*	wichtig	*important*
prima	*marvellous*	wirklich	*real(ly)*
toll	*great*	zahlreich	*numerous*
wunderbar	*wonderful*		
Lieblings-aufregend	*favourite exciting*	**Had a look** ☐ **Nearly there** ☐ **Nailed it** ☐	
spannend	*exciting, tense*	alle	*all*
ekelhaft	*disgusting*	eigen	*own*
enttäuscht	*disappointed*	ander–	*other*
langweilig	*boring*	einzig	*only*
schlecht	*bad*	allein	*alone*
schrecklich	*awful, terrible*	zusammen	*together*
		leise	*quiet*
Had a look ☐ **Nearly there** ☐ **Nailed it** ☐		lautlos	*soundless, silent*
		friedlich	*peaceful*
bequem	*comfortable*	ruhig	*calm*
dreckig	*dirty*	frei	*free, vacant*
flexibel	*flexible*	bereit	*ready*
gebrochen	*broken*	fertig	*ready*
gefährlich	*dangerous*	leicht	*easy, light*
geöffnet	*open*	schwierig	*difficult*
geschlossen	*closed*	schwer	*hard, heavy, difficult*
heiß	*hot*	erstaunlich	*astonishing*
kaputt	*broken*	unglaublich	*unbelievable*
kostenlos	*free (of charge)*	unvorstellbar	*unimaginable*
neu	*new*	erfreut	*pleased*
nötig	*necessary*	erstaunt	*astonished*
notwendig	*necessary*	überrascht	*surprised*
offen	*open*		
sauber	*clean*	**Had a look** ☐ **Nearly there** ☐ **Nailed it** ☐	
schmutzig	*dirty*		
teuer	*expensive*	**Common adverbs**	
umweltfeindlich	*environmentally damaging*	oben	*above, upstairs*
		unten	*below, downstairs*
umweltfreundlich	*environmentally friendly*	vorwärts	*forwards*
weich	*soft*	rückwärts	*backwards*
zerbrochen	*broken*	hier	*here*
		da	*there*
Had a look ☐ **Nearly there** ☐ **Nailed it** ☐		dort	*there*
		da drüben	*over there*
allgemein	*general*	irgendwo	*somewhere*
bestimmt	*definite*	draußen	*outside*
echt	*real(ly)*	mitten (in / auf / an / ...)	*in the middle of*
wahr	*true*	unterwegs	*en route, on the way*
richtig	*correct, right*	immer	*always*
falsch	*false*	oft	*often*
aktuell	*current*	regelmäßig	*regularly*
ehemalig	*old, former*	manchmal	*sometimes*
genau	*exact*	kaum	*barely, hardly*
gleich	*same*	nie	*never*
gültig	*valid*	neulich	*recently*
klar	*clear*	sofort	*immediately, straight away*
möglich	*possible*		
nützlich	*useful*	**Had a look** ☐ **Nearly there** ☐ **Nailed it** ☐	
typisch	*typical*		

High-frequency words

besonders	especially	statt	instead of
sehr	very	trotz	despite
wirklich	really	während	during
ziemlich	rather, quite	wegen	because of
zu	too		
immer noch	still		

Had a look ☐ Nearly there ☐ Nailed it ☐

fast	almost
genug	enough
jedoch	however
leider	unfortunately
vielleicht	perhaps
wahrscheinlich	probably
besser	better
gern	willingly
lieber	rather (preferably)
mehr	more
nur	only
schon	already
langsam	slowly
schnell	quickly

Colours

die Farbe	colour
blau	blue
braun	brown
dunkel	dark
gelb	yellow
grau	grey
grün	green
hell	light
lila	violet
rosa	pink
rot	red
schwarz	black
weiß	white

Had a look ☐ Nearly there ☐ Nailed it ☐

Had a look ☐ Nearly there ☐ Nailed it ☐

Prepositions

bis	until
durch	through
entlang	along
für	for
gegen	against
ohne	without
um	around
wider	against

Had a look ☐ Nearly there ☐ Nailed it ☐

aus	out of
außer	except
bei	at, with, next to
gegenüber	opposite
mit	with
nach	after
seit	since
von	from
zu	to
hin zu	towards

Had a look ☐ Nearly there ☐ Nailed it ☐

an	at
auf	on
hinter	behind
in	in, into
neben	next to
über	above, over
unter	beneath, under
vor	in front of
zwischen	between

Had a look ☐ Nearly there ☐ Nailed it ☐

Numbers

eins	one (1)
zwei	two (2)
drei	three (3)
vier	four (4)
fünf	five (5)
sechs	six (6)
sieben	seven (7)
acht	eight (8)
neun	nine (9)
zehn	ten (10)
elf	eleven (11)
zwölf	twelve (12)
dreizehn	thirteen (13)
vierzehn	fourteen (14)
fünfzehn	fifteen (15)
sechzehn	sixteen (16)
siebzehn	seventeen (17)
achtzehn	eighteen (18)
neunzehn	nineteen (19)
zwanzig	twenty (20)

Had a look ☐ Nearly there ☐ Nailed it ☐

einundzwanzig	twenty-one (21)
zweiundzwanzig	twenty-two (22)
dreiundzwanzig	twenty-three (23)
vierundzwanzig	twenty-four (24)
fünfundzwanzig	twenty-five (25)
sechsundzwanzig	twenty-six (26)
siebenundzwanzig	twenty-seven (27)
achtundzwanzig	twenty-eight (28)

High-frequency words

neunundzwanzig	twenty-nine (29)
dreißig	thirty (30)

Had a look ☐ **Nearly there** ☐ **Nailed it** ☐

vierzig	forty (40)
fünfzig	fifty (50)
sechzig	sixty (60)
siebzig	seventy (70)
achtzig	eighty (80)
neunzig	ninety (90)
hundert	(one) hundred (100)
einhundert	(one) hundred (100)
hunderteins	one hundred and one (101)
hundertzwanzig	one hundred and twenty (120)
zweihundert	two hundred (200)
tausend	one thousand (1,000)
eintausend	one thousand (1,000)
tausendeinhundert	one thousand one hundred (1,100)
elfhundert	one thousand one hundred (1,100)
zweitausend	two thousand (2,000)
(eine) Million	one million (1,000,000)
zwei Millionen	two million (2,000,000)

Had a look ☐ **Nearly there** ☐ **Nailed it** ☐

erster/erste/erstes	first
zweiter/zweite/zweites	second
elfter/elfte/elftes	eleventh
einundzwanzigster/ einundzwanzigste/ einundzwanzigstes	twenty-first

Had a look ☐ **Nearly there** ☐ **Nailed it** ☐

Quantities and measures

viele	many
mehrere	several
genug	enough
ein bisschen	a little
ein Drittel	a third (of)
ein Dutzend	a dozen
eine Dose	a tin (of)
eine Flasche	a bottle (of)
ein Glas	a jar (of)
eine Kiste	a box (of)
eine Packung	a packet (of)
eine Schachtel	a box (of)
eine Scheibe	a slice (of)
ein Stück	a piece (of)
eine Tafel	a bar (of)
eine Tüte	a bag (of)

Had a look ☐ **Nearly there** ☐ **Nailed it** ☐

Some useful connecting words

aber	but
also	so
anstatt	instead
auch	also
außerdem	additionally, moreover
dafür	instead
danach	afterwards
dann	then
deshalb	for this reason
deswegen	for this reason
jedoch	however
nachher	afterwards, later
oder	or
übrigens	by the way, moreover
und	and
vorher	beforehand
weil	because
zuerst	first of all

Had a look ☐ **Nearly there** ☐ **Nailed it** ☐

Time expressions

der Tag(e)	day
der Morgen(–)	morning
der Vormittag(e)	morning
der Nachmittag(e)	afternoon
der Abend(e)	evening
die Nacht (Nächte)	night
Mitternacht	midnight
die Woche(n)	week
das Wochenende(n)	weekend
gestern	yesterday
heute	today
morgen	tomorrow
morgen früh	tomorrow morning
übermorgen	the day after tomorrow
vorgestern	the day before yesterday
die Minute(n)	minute

Had a look ☐ **Nearly there** ☐ **Nailed it** ☐

ab	from
ab und zu	now and then
von Zeit zu Zeit	from time to time
am Anfang	at the start
bald	soon
früh	early
heutzutage	nowadays
immer	always
immer noch	still
jetzt	now
meistens	mostly
nächst–	next
pünktlich	on time
rechtzeitig	on time

9

High-frequency words

seit	since
sofort	immediately
spät	late
später	later
täglich	every day, daily
wöchentlich	weekly

Had a look ☐ Nearly there ☐ Nailed it ☐

Times of day

(um) ein Uhr	(at) one o'clock
13.00 Uhr	one o'clock (1 p.m.)
dreizehn Uhr	one o'clock (1 p.m.)
21.00 Uhr	nine o'clock (9 p.m.)
einundzwanzig Uhr	nine o'clock (9 p.m.)
neun Uhr abends	nine o'clock in the evening
genau um 14.00 Uhr	at exactly two o'clock (2 p.m.)
genau um vierzehn Uhr	at exactly two o'clock (2 p.m.)
gegen ... Uhr	at about ... o'clock
ungefähr um ... Uhr	at about ... o'clock
es ist 3.05 Uhr	it is five past three
es ist drei Uhr fünf	it is five past three
fünf vor drei	five to three
zehn nach vier	ten past four
zehn vor vier	ten to four
Viertel vor sechs	quarter to six
Viertel nach sieben	quarter past seven
halb elf	half past ten

Had a look ☐ Nearly there ☐ Nailed it ☐

Days of the week

Montag	Monday
Dienstag	Tuesday
Mittwoch	Wednesday
Donnerstag	Thursday
Freitag	Friday
Samstag	Saturday
Sonnabend	Saturday
Sonntag	Sunday
(am) Montag	(on) Monday
(am) Montagvormittag	(on) Monday morning
(am) Montagabend	(on) Monday evening
montags	on Mondays
jeden Montag	every Monday

Had a look ☐ Nearly there ☐ Nailed it ☐

Months and seasons

der Monat(e)	month
Januar	January
Februar	February
März	March
April	April
Mai	May
Juni	June
Juli	July
August	August
September	September
Oktober	October
November	November
Dezember	December
die Jahreszeit(en)	season
(im) Frühling	(in) spring
(im) Sommer	(in) summer
(im) Herbst	(in) autumn
(im) Winter	(in) winter

Had a look ☐ Nearly there ☐ Nailed it ☐

Question words

wann?	when?
warum?	why?
was für?	what sort of?
was?	what?
wen? wem?	whom?
wer?	who?, whom?
wessen?	whose?
wie viel(e)?	how much?, how many?
wie?	how?
wo?	where?

Had a look ☐ Nearly there ☐ Nailed it ☐

Other useful expressions

Es gibt ...	There is/are ...
Hier gibt es ...	Here is/are ...
Man darf nicht ...	You are not allowed to ...
Man muss ...	You/one must ...
Wie schreibt man das?	How do you spell that?
Was bedeutet das?	What does that mean?
Noch einmal?	Once again?
Ich verstehe nicht.	I don't understand.
Ich weiß es nicht.	I don't know.
Es geht mir gut.	I'm fine.
Ich bin satt.	I'm full. / I've had enough (to eat).
Natürlich!	Of course!
In Ordnung!	OK! (in agreement)
Mit Vergnügen!	With pleasure!
Viel Glück!	Good luck!
Schade!	Too bad! / What a shame!
Genug davon!	That's enough!

Had a look ☐ Nearly there ☐ Nailed it ☐

Opinions

Meiner Meinung nach ...	In my opinion ...
Ich denke, dass ...	In my opinion ...
Persönlich ...	Personally, ...
Das interessiert mich nicht.	That doesn't interest me / appeal to me.
Es ärgert mich.	It annoys me.

High-frequency words

Es bringt mich zum Lachen.	It makes me laugh.	die Schweiz	Switzerland
Es gefällt mir.	I like it.	Schottland	Scotland
Es ist mir egal.	I don't mind.	Spanien	Spain
Es kommt darauf an.	It depends.	die Türkei	Turkey
Es lohnt sich nicht.	It's not worth it.	die USA	the United States
Es macht nichts.	It doesn't matter.	die Vereinigten Staaten	the United States
		Wales	Wales

Had a look ☐ Nearly there ☐ Nailed it ☐   Had a look ☐ Nearly there ☐ Nailed it ☐

Other useful words

ja	yes	**Continents**	
nein	no	Afrika	Africa
das	that	Asien	Asia
etwas	something	Australien	Australia
ob	whether, if	Europa	Europe
wenn	if, when	Nordamerika	North America
wie	as, like	Südamerika	South America

Had a look ☐ Nearly there ☐ Nailed it ☐

alle	everyone
jeder	everybody
jemand	someone
zum Beispiel	for example

Nationalities

Amerikaner(in)	American
amerikanisch	American
Belgier(in)	Belgian
belgisch	Belgian
Brite/Britin	British
britisch	British
Däne/Dänin	Danish
dänisch	Danish
Deutsche(r)	German
deutsch	German
Engländer(in)	English
englisch	English
Franzose/Französin	French
französisch	French
Grieche/Griechin	Greek
griechisch	Greek
Inder(in)	Indian
indisch	Indian
Ire/Irin	Irish
irisch	Irish

Had a look ☐ Nearly there ☐ Nailed it ☐

das Ding(e)	thing
die Sache(n)	thing
der Gegenstand (-stände)	object
die Form(en)	shape
die Art(en)	type
die Weise(n)	way
die Nummer(n)	number
das Mal(e)	time
die Zahl(en)	figure, number
die Mitte(n)	middle
das Ende(n)	end
Herr ...	Mr ...
Frau ...	Mrs ...

Had a look ☐ Nearly there ☐ Nailed it ☐

Countries

Belgien	Belgium
Dänemark	Denmark
Deutschland	Germany
England	England
Frankreich	France
Griechenland	Greece
Großbritannien	Great Britain
Indien	India
Irland	Ireland
Italien	Italy
die Niederlande	the Netherlands
Österreich	Austria
Polen	Poland
Russland	Russia

Had a look ☐ Nearly there ☐ Nailed it ☐

Italiener(in)	Italian
italienisch	Italian
Niederländer(in)	Dutch
niederländisch	Dutch
Österreicher(in)	Austrian
österreichisch	Austrian
Pakistani	Pakistani
pakistanisch	Pakistani
Russe/Russin	Russian
russisch	Russian
Schotte/Schottin	Scottish
schottisch	Scottish
Schweizer(in)	Swiss

High-frequency words

schweizerisch	*Swiss*
Spanier(in)	*Spanish*
spanisch	*Spanish*
Türke/Türkin	*Turkish*
türkisch	*Turkish*
Waliser(in)	*Welsh*
walisisch	*Welsh*

Had a look ☐   **Nearly there** ☐   **Nailed it** ☐

Places

Bayern	*Bavaria*
Köln	*Cologne*
München	*Munich*
Wien	*Vienna*
die Alpen	*the Alps*
der Schwarzwald	*the Black Forest*
die Donau	*the Danube*
der Rhein	*the Rhine*
der Bodensee	*Lake Constance*
der Ärmelkanal	*the English Channel*
der Eurotunnel	*the Channel Tunnel*

Had a look ☐   **Nearly there** ☐   **Nailed it** ☐

Social conventions

Guten Tag!	*Good day!*
Guten Abend!	*Good evening!*
Gute Nacht!	*Good night!*
Grüß Gott!	*Hello!*
Auf Wiedersehen!	*Goodbye!*
Bis später!	*See you later!*
Bis bald!	*See you soon!*
Bis morgen!	*See you tomorrow!*
Entschuldigung!	*Excuse me!*
Hilfe!	*Help!*
Wie bitte?	*I beg your pardon?*
Alles Gute!	*All the best!*
Mit bestem Gruß	*Best wishes*
bitte	*please*
danke schön	*thank you very much*
Bitte schön!	*You're welcome!*

Had a look ☐   **Nearly there** ☐   **Nailed it** ☐

Language used in dialogues and messages

Rufen Sie mich an!	*Call me! (formal)*
Ruf mich an!	*Call me! (informal)*
Kann ich etwas ausrichten?	*Can I take a message?*
Ich verbinde Sie.	*I will put you through.*
Ich höre zu.	*I'm listening.*
Ich bin gleich wieder da.	*I'll be right back.*
Warten Sie einen Moment.	*Wait a moment.*

Betreff …	*Regarding …*
In Bezug auf …	*Further to / Following …*
Zu Händen von …	*For the attention of …*

Had a look ☐   **Nearly there** ☐   **Nailed it** ☐

das Telefon(e)	*telephone*
der Hörer(–)	*receiver (telephone)*
der Ton (Töne)	*tone*
die Vorwahl(en)	*area code*
die Telefonnummer wählen	*to dial the number*
im Gespräch mit	*in communication with*
am Apparat	*on the line / speaking*
der Augenblick(e)	*moment*
für jetzt	*for the moment*
falsche Nummer	*wrong number*
die SMS(–)	*text message*
simsen	*to text*
die E-Mail(s)	*email*
gesandt von	*sent by*
eigentlich	*in fact*

Had a look ☐   **Nearly there** ☐   **Nailed it** ☐

Kapitel 1 Wörter

Words I should know for speaking and writing activities

Schulfächer	School subjects
Sprachen	languages
Deutsch	German
Englisch	English
Französisch	French
Spanisch	Spanish
Naturwissenschaft(en)	science(s)
Biologie	biology
Chemie	chemistry
Physik	physics
Mathe(matik)	math(ematic)s
Informatik	ICT
Geschichte	history
Erdkunde	geography
Politik	politics
Gesellschaft	sociology
Wirtschaft	economics
Kunst	art
Musik	music
Theater	drama
Religion	RE
Sport	PE, sport
das Wahlfach	optional subject
das Pflichtfach	compulsory subject

Had a look ☐ Nearly there ☐ Nailed it ☐

Kleidung	Clothes
Ich trage (nie) ...	I (never) wear ...
einen Rock	a skirt
eine Jeans	jeans
eine Hose	trousers
eine Jacke	a jacket
eine Krawatte	a tie
ein Hemd	a shirt
ein Kleid	a dress
ein T-Shirt	a T-shirt
Sportschuhe	trainers
Schuhe	shoes

Had a look ☐ Nearly there ☐ Nailed it ☐

Schulsachen	School items
Was hast du (für das neue Schuljahr / die neunte Klasse) gekauft?	What have you bought (for the new school year / Year 9)?
Ich habe ... gekauft.	I bought ...
einen Bleistift	a pencil
einen Füller	a fountain pen
einen Kuli	a ballpoint pen
einen Radiergummi	a rubber
einen Taschenrechner	a calculator
ein Etui	a pencil case
ein Lineal	a ruler
Filzstifte	felt-tip pens

Had a look ☐ Nearly there ☐ Nailed it ☐

Das neue Schuljahr	The new school year
In der neunten Klasse freue ich mich (nicht) auf ...	I'm (not) looking forward to ... in Year 9.
den Druck	the pressure
die Klassenfahrt	the class trip
das Zeugnis	the report
die Hausaufgaben	the homework
die (Sport-)AG(s)	the sport club(s)
die Klassenarbeiten	the tests
die Prüfungen	the exams
neue Fächer	new subjects
meine Freunde/Freundinnen	my friends
die Noten	the grades
am meisten	mostly
total	totally
(echt) sehr	(really) very
weniger	less
(gar) nicht	not (at all)
nie	never
langweilig	boring
stressig	stressful
schwierig	difficult
interessant	interesting
einfach	simple

Had a look ☐ Nearly there ☐ Nailed it ☐

Ein Schultag	A school day
Was hat (die Klasse 9) in der (ersten) Stunde am (Montag)?	What does (Year 9) have in the (first) lesson on (Monday)?
zweite(n)	second
dritte(n)	third
vierte(n)	fourth
fünfte(n)	fifth
sechste(n)	sixth
siebte(n)	seventh
Die Schule beginnt um ...	School starts at ...
Die Schule endet um ...	School ends at ...
die (kleine) Pause	(short) break
die Mittagspause	lunch break
Wir haben ... Stunden pro Tag.	We have ... lessons per day.
Jede Stunde dauert ... Minuten.	Each lesson lasts ... minutes.
Ich habe vier Stunden pro Woche (Erdkunde).	I have four lessons of (geography) per week.

K 1

13

Kapitel 1 Wörter

Ich habe viermal pro Woche (Mathe).	I have (maths) four times a week.
Mein Lieblingsfach ist (Physik).	My favourite subject is (physics).

Had a look ☐ Nearly there ☐ Nailed it ☐

Fragen stellen / *Asking questions*

Wann?	When?
Wie viele?	How many?
Um wie viel Uhr?	At what time?
Wie oft?	How often?
Was?	What?
Ist (Mathe) dein Lieblingsfach?	Is (maths) your favourite subject?
Warum?	Why?
Welches Fach?	Which subject?
Wie?	How?
Wer?	Who?

Had a look ☐ Nearly there ☐ Nailed it ☐

Die Schulordnung / *School rules*

der Computerraum	ICT room
der Schulhof	playground
die Aula	assembly hall
die Bibliothek	library
die Kantine	canteen
die Sporthalle	sports hall
das Klassenzimmer	classroom
das Labor	lab(oratory)
das Lehrerzimmer	staff room
die Toiletten	toilets

Had a look ☐ Nearly there ☐ Nailed it ☐

Wir dürfen nicht …	We are not allowed to …
Wir dürfen weder … noch …	We are allowed neither … nor …
schlagen	to hit
mobben	to bully
(auf dem Schulgelände) rauchen	to smoke (in the school grounds)
essen	to eat
trinken	to drink
Sportschuhe tragen	wear trainers
Handball spielen	play handball
Wir dürfen keine Schimpfwörter sagen.	We are not allowed to use swear words.
Wir dürfen keinen Kaugummi kauen.	We are not allowed to chew gum.
Wir müssen …	We have to …
den Müll trennen	separate the rubbish
immer Hochdeutsch sprechen	always speak standard German
ruhig sein	be quiet
höflich sein	be polite
pünktlich sein	be punctual
respektvoll sein	be respectful

Had a look ☐ Nearly there ☐ Nailed it ☐

zu	too
sehr	very
ziemlich	rather, quite
streng	strict
ärgerlich	annoying
nervig	irritating
(un)gerecht	(un)just
(un)fair	(un)fair
locker	casual, informal

Had a look ☐ Nearly there ☐ Nailed it ☐

Das deutsche Schulsystem / *The German school system*

Ich besuche …	I go to …
die Grundschule	primary school
die Gesamtschule	comprehensive school
die Hauptschule	a type of secondary modern school
die Realschule	a type of secondary modern school
das Gymnasium	grammar school
die Oberstufe	sixth form
die Ganztagsschule	all-day school
das Internat	boarding school
der Mittlere Schulabschluss	German equivalent of GCSEs
das Abitur	German equivalent of A levels
gemischt	mixed
privat	private
staatlich	state
Man hat …	We have …
(k)einen Stundenplan	no / a timetable
(k)eine Schuluniform	no / a school uniform
(keine) Hausaufgaben	(no) homework
Man hat tolle / keine Computerräume.	We have great / no ICT rooms.
Die Schule ist prima ausgestattet.	The school is very well equipped.
Die Schule ist schlecht ausgestattet.	The school is very well badly equipped.
Ich bin sitzen geblieben.	I repeated the year.
Ich muss das Jahr wiederholen.	I have to repeat the year.

Had a look ☐ Nearly there ☐ Nailed it ☐

Eine Klassenfahrt / *A class trip*

Was werden wir am (Mittwoch) machen?	What will we do on (Wednesday)?
Ich werde …	I will …

Kapitel 1 Wörter

Deutsch sprechen	*speak German*	Ich bin bei der Prüfung durchgefallen.	*I failed the exam.*
einen Schultag erleben	*experience a school day*	Wir haben den Erfolg (im Restaurant) gefeiert.	*We celebrated the success (in a restaurant).*
einen Tagesausflug machen	*go on a day trip*	Meine Eltern waren stolz auf mich.	*My parents were proud of me.*
eine Fahrradtour machen	*go on a cycling tour*	Ich habe (ein Computerspiel) als Belohnung bekommen.	*I received (a computer game) as a reward.*
ein Kunstprojekt machen	*do an art project*	Es gab ein Foto in der Zeitung.	*There was a photo in the newspaper.*
den Abend bei einer Gastfamilie verbringen	*spend the evening with a host family*	Ich war / Wir waren … glücklich	*I was / We were … happy*
das (Zirkus-)Museum besuchen	*visit the (circus) museum*	erfolgreich	*successful*
den Freizeitpark besuchen	*visit the theme park*	Das war ein tolles Erlebnis.	*That was a great experience.*
die Sehenswürdigkeiten besichtigen	*visit the sights*		

Had a look ☐ Nearly there ☐ Nailed it ☐

ins Hallenbad / Freibad gehen	*go to the indoor / outdoor swimming pool*
in der Altstadt bummeln	*stroll around the old town*
Andenken kaufen	*buy souvenirs*
(wieder) nach Hause fahren	*go home (again)*
Es wird … kosten.	*It will cost …*
Das wird Spaß machen.	*That will be fun.*
Heimweh haben	*to be homesick*
reisekrank sein	*to be travel sick*
Die Reise hat … gedauert.	*The journey lasted …*
Das war eine Katastrophe!	*That was a catastrophe!*
Es gab (kein) WLAN.	*There was (no) Wi-Fi.*

Had a look ☐ Nearly there ☐ Nailed it ☐

Erfolge feiern / *Celebrating successes*

Welchen Erfolg hast du in der Schule gefeiert?	*What success have you celebrated at school?*
Unsere Schule hat großen Erfolg gehabt.	*Our school has had great success.*
Unsere Mannschaft hat einen Preis gewonnen.	*Our team won a prize.*
Ich habe an … teilgenommen.	*I took part in …*
dem Spendenlauf	*the charity run*
der Spendenschwimm-Aktion	*the charity swim*
Wir haben ein Theaterstück aufgeführt.	*We put on a play.*
Wir haben neue Leute kennengelernt.	*We got to know new people.*
Wir haben beim Schulwettbewerb mitgemacht.	*We took part in the school competition.*
Es gab großen Applaus.	*There was great applause.*
Ich bin mit vielen Medaillen zurückgekommen.	*I came back with lots of medals.*

Kapitel 1 Wörter

Extra words I should know for reading and listening activities

Schularbeit — *School work*

die Durchschnittsnote	*average grade*
ausgezeichnet	*excellent*
befriedigend	*fair*
ausreichend	*satisfactory*
mangelhaft	*poor*
ungenügend	*unsatisfactory*
stark	*strong, good at (subject)*
schwach	*weak, bad at (subject)*
begabt	*gifted*
aufpassen	*to pay attention*
üben	*to practise*
verbessern	*to improve*
(eine Prüfung) bestehen*	*to pass (an exam)*
der Fortschritt(e)	*progress*
die Leistung(en)	*achievement*
die Strafarbeit(en)	*written punishment, lines*
die Geisteswissenschaften	*humanities (subjects)*
die Zeitverschwendung	*waste of time*
das Trimester(–)	*term*
die Zukunft	*future*

Had a look ☐ Nearly there ☐ Nailed it ☐

In der Schule — *At school*

die Tafel	*board (e.g. whiteboard)*
das Sprachlabor	*language lab*
die Rezeption	*reception*
der Sportplatz(–plätze)	*sports field*
der Anschluss	*connection (e.g. internet)*
das Netzwerk(e)	*network*
die Renovierung(en)	*renovation*
die Erlaubnis	*permission*

Had a look ☐ Nearly there ☐ Nailed it ☐

Auf Austausch — *On an exchange*

der Austausch	*exchange*
der Ausweis	*identity card*
das Erlebnis(se)	*experience*
die Gegend(en)	*area, region*
die Grenze(n)	*border*
der Reisepass	*passport*
die Abschiedsparty(s)	*farewell party*
die Willkommensparty(s)	*welcome party*
eine Reise wert sein	*to be worth a trip*
Angst vor … haben	*to be afraid / scared of …*
besuchen	*to visit*
sich melden bei	*to get in touch with*
mitbringen**	*to bring (with you)*
mitmachen**	*to join in, to take part in*
stattfinden	*to take place*
übernachten	*to stay, to spend the night*
überqueren	*to cross*
wandern	*to go hiking*

Had a look ☐ Nearly there ☐ Nailed it ☐

⭐ *Watch out for false friends! To say 'to pass an exam' in German, you don't use *passieren* (which means 'to happen'). Instead, you need the verb *bestehen*:

Ich hoffe, ich werde meine Prüfungen bestehen.
I hope I will pass my exams.

Note that *bestehen* is irregular in the perfect tense:

Ich habe meine Prüfungen bestanden.
I passed my exams.

⭐ **Break unfamiliar verbs down into their component parts to work out their meaning:

mitmachen: mit + machen → to join in, to take part (literally: to do (something) with)

mitbringen: mit + bringen → to bring with (you)

mitnehmen: mit + nehmen → to take with (you)

Kapitel 2 Wörter

Words I should know for speaking and writing activities

Freizeitaktivitäten	**Leisure activities**
die Freizeit	leisure time, free time
Briefmarken sammeln	to collect stamps
Plüschtiere sammeln	to collect soft toys
Sport machen	to do sport
Sport treiben	to do sport
Fußball spielen	to play football
Hockey spielen	to play hockey
Basketball spielen	to play basketball
Schach spielen	to play chess
Karten spielen	to play cards
am Computer spielen	to play on the computer
Computerspiele spielen	to play computer games
im Internet surfen	to surf on the internet
im Internet chatten	to chat on the internet
mit Freunden reden	to chat with friends
mit Freunden chillen	to chill with friends
Freunde treffen	to meet friends
Zeit mit dem besten Freund/der besten Freundin verbringen	to spend time with your best friend
ins Kino gehen	to go to the cinema
in die Stadt gehen	to go into town
abends fernsehen	to watch TV in the evening
am Wochenende Videos gucken	to watch videos at the weekend
Filme sehen	to watch films
die Nachrichten sehen	to watch the news

Had a look ☐   Nearly there ☐   Nailed it ☐

Musik machen	to make music
Radio hören	to listen to the radio
Bücher lesen	to read books
faulenzen	to chill, to laze about
nichts tun	to do nothing
Ich bin …	I am …
(nicht) sehr	(not) very
ziemlich	quite
ein bisschen	a bit
(gar) nicht	not (at all)
sportlich	sporty
musikalisch	musical
faul	lazy
abenteuerlustig	adventurous

Had a look ☐   Nearly there ☐   Nailed it ☐

Instrumente	**Instruments**
die Blockflöte	recorder
die Flöte	flute
die Geige	violin
die (elektrische) Gitarre	(electric) guitar
die Klarinette	clarinet
die Trompete	trumpet
das Keyboard	keyboard
das Klavier	piano
das Saxofon	saxophone
das Schlagzeug	drums
Ich spiele kein Instrument.	I don't play an instrument.

Had a look ☐   Nearly there ☐   Nailed it ☐

Bücher	**Books**
gedruckt	printed
das Buch (Bücher)	book
das gedruckte Buch	printed book
die Biografie(n)	biography
der Comic(s)	comic book
der Fantasyroman(e)	fantasy novel
die Horrorgeschichte(n)	horror story
die Komödie(n)	comedy
der Krimi(s)	detective / crime story
die Liebesgeschichte(n)	love story
das Science-Fiction-Buch(–Bücher)	sci-fi-book
der Thriller(–)	thriller

Had a look ☐   Nearly there ☐   Nailed it ☐

die Zeitung(en)	newspaper
die Zeitschrift(en)	magazine
das Magazin(e)	magazine
die Illustrierte(n)	(glossy) magazine
das Blog(s)	blog
das E-Book(s)	e-book
das Taschenbuch (–bücher)	paperback book
Ich lese (oft / nie) Taschenbücher …	I (often / never) read paperbacks …
auf meinem Tablet / E-Reader	on my tablet / e-reader
auf einem elektronischen Gerät	on an electronic device
im Bett	in bed
in meinem Zimmer	in my room
im Bus	on the bus
der Akku	rechargeable battery
der Bildschirm	screen

Had a look ☐   Nearly there ☐   Nailed it ☐

Musik	**Music**
Ich interessiere mich für viele Musikrichtungen.	I'm interested in lots of types of music.
die Musiksammlung	music collection
Ich höre (nicht) gern …	I (don't) like listening to …
Ich höre lieber …	I prefer to listen to …

17

Kapitel 2 Wörter

Ich höre am liebsten …	I like listening to … best of all.
klassische Musik	classical music
Opernmusik	opera
Popmusik	pop music
Reggae	reggae
R&B-Musik	R&B
Rapmusik	rap
Heavy Metal-Musik	heavy metal
Country-und-Western-Musik	country and western
Jazzmusik	jazz
Livemusik	live music

Had a look ☐ Nearly there ☐ Nailed it ☐

Ich höre Musik auf meinem …	I listen to music on my …
Handy / Smartphone	mobile phone / smartphone
Laptop / Tablet	laptop / tablet
Musik herunterladen / downloaden	to download music
Das ist praktisch.	That's practical.
Ich spiele seit (einem Jahr) Gitarre.	I have been playing guitar for (a year).
Ich downloade alles auf mein Tablet.	I download everything onto my tablet.
Das spart so viel Platz.	That saves so much space.
Der Ton (auf einem Tablet) ist nicht gut.	The sound (on a tablet) is not good.
Die Qualität ist fantastisch.	The quality is fantastic.
Die Eintrittskarten sind zu teuer.	The entry tickets are too expensive.
Ich gebe kein Geld für (Musik) aus.	I don't spend any money on (music).
Das ist ein tolles Gefühl.	That's a great feeling.

Had a look ☐ Nearly there ☐ Nailed it ☐

Film und Fernsehen / Film and television

der Film(e)	film, movie
der Actionfilm(e)	action movie
der Fantasyfilm(e)	fantasy film
der Horrorfilm(e)	horror film
die Komödie(n)	comedy
der Krimi(s)	detective / crime film
der Liebesfilm(e)	romance
der Science-Fiction-Film(e)	sci-fi film
der Thriller(–)	thriller
der Zeichentrickfilm(e)	cartoon
Ich sehe gern fern.	I like watching TV.
der Zuschauer(–)	viewer
das Fernsehen	television
die Fernsehsendung(en)	TV programme
die Serie(n)	series
die Gameshow(s)	game show
die Realityshow(s)	reality show
die Dokumentation(en)	documentary
die Nachrichten (pl)	the news
Ich finde (Serien) (blöd).	I find (series) (silly).
Ich habe (die Sendung / den Film) (großartig) gefunden.	I found (the programme / film) (great).

Had a look ☐ Nearly there ☐ Nailed it ☐

Die Sendung / Der Film / Die Handlung war …	The programme / film / plot, story line was …
Die Schauspieler waren …	The actors were …
(un)realistisch	(un)realistic
schwach	weak
enttäuschend	disappointing
überzeugend	convincing
humorvoll	humorous, amusing
(Der Film) macht keinen Sinn.	(The film) doesn't make sense.
Ich bin von (der Sendung / dem Film) (nicht) begeistert, weil …	I'm (not) enthusiastic about (the programme / film) because …
Ich empfehle (die Sendung / den Film), weil …	I recommend (the programme / film) because …

Had a look ☐ Nearly there ☐ Nailed it ☐

Sport / Sport

Ski fahren	to go skiing
snowboarden	to go snowboarding
rodeln	to sledge, to toboggan
eislaufen	to ice skate
Curling spielen	to do curling
Nordic Walking machen	to go Nordic walking
wandern	to hike
klettern	to climb
schwimmen	to swim
Fahrrad / Rad fahren	to cycle
Handball spielen	to play handball
Fußball spielen	to play football
Tennis spielen	to play tennis

Had a look ☐ Nearly there ☐ Nailed it ☐

Ich spiele gern (Fußball).	I like playing (football).
Ich turne seit (fünf Jahren).	I have been doing gymnastics for (five years).
Ich mache (nicht) gern (Nordic Walking).	I (don't) like doing (Nordic walking).
Ich habe mit (sechs) Jahren angefangen, Tennis zu spielen.	I started to play tennis when I was (six) years old.

Kapitel 2 Wörter

Ich habe (Rollschuhlaufen) im Alter von (sechs) Jahren gelernt.	I learned to (roller skate) at the age of (six).
Ich habe schon (Golf) ausprobiert.	I have already tried (golf).
Ich würde (nie) (Skateboard fahren).	I would (never) do (skateboarding).
Ich trainiere (jeden Tag) mit Freunden im Verein.	I train with friends at the club (every day).
die Bodenübung	floor work
der Hochweitsprung	high long jump
der 100-Meter-Lauf	100-metre sprint
das Ringen	wrestling
das Schwingen	another type of wrestling
das Steinheben	stone lifting
das Steinstoßen	stone tossing
der Weitsprung	long jump

Had a look ☐   **Nearly there** ☐   **Nailed it** ☐

Feste und Feiertage — *Festivals and celebrations*

am 24. Dezember (usw.)	on the 24th December (etc.)
feiern	to celebrate
(Zeit) verbringen	to spend (time)
stattfinden	to take place
zu Ostern	at Easter
zu Weihnachten	at Christmas
der Feiertag(e)	public holiday
der Festzug(-züge)	procession
der Karneval	carnival
der Fasching	carnival
der Maibaum(-bäume)	may pole
die Fete(n)	party
das Fest(e)	festival, fair
das Feuerwerk(e)	fireworks (pl)
das Geschenk(e)	present
das Volksfest(e)	(traditional) fair

Had a look ☐   **Nearly there** ☐   **Nailed it** ☐

Es gibt ...	There is/are ...
Reden / Feste / Konzerte	speeches / celebrations / concerts
Musik / Tanz / tolle Kostüme	music / dancing / great costumes
Proteste / ein Feuerwerk	protests / fireworks
Ich bin (auf den Weihnachtsmarkt) gegangen.	I went (to the Christmas market).
Das war der Höhepunkt des Jahres.	That was the highlight of the year.
Die Stimmung war super.	The atmosphere was great.
Ich habe (Lebkuchen) gegessen / gekauft.	I ate / bought (gingerbread).
Am Ende des Tages war ich (völlig satt / müde).	At the end of the day I was (totally full / tired).
Ich würde gern (auf einen Markt in England) gehen.	I would like to go (to a market in England).
Es würde mich interessieren, ... zu sehen.	I would be interested in seeing ...
Ich könnte über ... lernen.	I could learn about ...
Ich werde nächstes Jahr (in England) feiern.	Next year I will celebrate (in England).

Had a look ☐   **Nearly there** ☐   **Nailed it** ☐

19

Kapitel 2 Wörter

Extra words I should know for reading and listening activities

Freizeit	**Leisure time**
das Brettspiel	board game
die Festplatte	hard drive
der Fotoapparat	camera
die Freizeitbeschäftigung	leisure activity
die Kopfhörer (pl)	headphones
der Lautsprecher(-)	(loud)speaker
der Rhythmus	rhythm
die Spielkonsole	games console
die Unterhaltung	entertainment
das Vinyl	vinyl (records)
die Volksmusik	folk music
bequem	comfortable
entspannend	relaxing
griffbereit	handy
kostenlos	free (of charge)
gratis	free (of charge)
lebhaft	lively
unhandlich	unwieldy
verändern	to change
stundenlang	for hours

Had a look ☐ Nearly there ☐ Nailed it ☐

Film und Fernsehen	**Film and television**
die Atmosphäre	atmosphere
die Fernbedienung(en)	remote control
die Kurzfassung(en)	summary
die Originalfassung(en)	original version
das Satellitenfernsehen	satellite TV
die Spezialeffekte (pl)	special effects
die Szene	scene
das Thema	theme, topic
glaubhaft	credible
hervorragend	excellent
humoristisch	humorous
komisch	funny, strange
satirisch	satirical

Had a look ☐ Nearly there ☐ Nailed it ☐

Sport	**Sport**
die Sportart	(type of) sport
der Extremsport	extreme sport
das Bergsteigen	mountaineering
das Fallschirmspringen	parachuting
das Fechten	fencing
der Federball	badminton
die Leichtathletik	(field and track) athletics
das Radrennen	cycle racing
das Rudern	rowing
das Turnier	tournament
der Wettkampf	competition
der Gegner	opponent
die Ausdauer	stamina, endurance
die Kraft	strength
die Schnelligkeit	speed
die Eisbahn	ice rink
die Kletterwand	climbing wall
der Teamgeist	team spirit
ausprobieren	to try (out)
überholen	to overtake
werfen	to throw
gefährlich	dangerous

Had a look ☐ Nearly there ☐ Nailed it ☐

Feste und Feiertage	**Celebrations and holidays**
der Arbeitstag	working day
Karfreitag	Good Friday
Ostermontag	Easter Monday
der Osterhase	Easter bunny
das Osterei	Easter egg
die Wiedervereinigung*	reunification
die Vorweihnachtszeit	pre-Christmas period
Heiligabend	Christmas Eve
der Weihnachtsbaum	Christmas tree
der Imbiss	snack
die Wollmütze	woolly hat
das Spielzeug	toy
das Kaufhaus	department store
das Angebot	offer
bieten	to offer
Geld ausgeben	to spend money
genießen	to enjoy
gesetzlich	statutory
die Ruhe	peace, rest

Had a look ☐ Nearly there ☐ Nailed it ☐

---

*Don't be daunted by long, tricky-looking words. Look carefully at the words they are made up of and try to work out the meaning based on the words you know.

die Wiedervereinigung

You know that *wieder* means 'again' and *der Verein* is 'club' (i.e. somewhere where people come together), so *die Wiedervereinigung* is literally 'the coming together again', or 'reunification'.

Man feiert die Wiedervereinigung Deutschlands am 3. Oktober. We celebrate the reunification of Germany on 3 October.

Kapitel 3 Wörter

Words I should know for speaking and writing activities

Charaktereigen-schaften	*Personal characteristics*
Er/Sie ist …	*He/She is …*
abenteuerlustig	*adventurous*
aktiv	*active*
cool	*cool*
dynamisch	*dynamic*
fleißig	*hard-working*
frech	*cheeky*
freundlich	*friendly*
intelligent	*intelligent*
kreativ	*creative*
langweilig	*boring*
locker	*laid-back*
lustig	*funny*
modisch	*fashionable*
nett	*nice*
originell	*original*
selbstbewusst	*self-confident*
sportlich	*sporty*
unterhaltsam	*entertaining*

Had a look ☐ **Nearly there** ☐ **Nailed it** ☐

Aussehen	*Appearance*
Sie hat (braune) Haare.	*She has (brown) hair.*
blond	*blonde*
braun	*brown*
grau	*grey*
schwarz	*black*
rotbraun	*auburn*
kurz	*short*
lang	*long*
glatt	*straight*
dunkel	*dark*
hell	*light*
Er/Sie hat (blaue) Augen.	*He/She has (blue) eyes.*
Er/Sie trägt …	*He/She wears …*
eine Brille	*glasses*
eine Sonnenbrille	*sunglasses*
Er hat einen Bart.	*He has a beard.*
Sie hat Sommersprossen.	*She has freckles.*
Er/Sie ist …	*He/She is …*
hübsch	*pretty*
schlank	*slim*

Had a look ☐ **Nearly there** ☐ **Nailed it** ☐

Wie ist ein guter Freund/eine gute Freundin?	*What makes a good friend?*
Ein guter Freund/Eine gute Freundin …	*A good friend …*
hat immer Zeit für mich	*always has time for me*
ist sympathisch	*is nice*
unterstützt mich immer	*always supports me*
muss hilfsbereit sein	*must be helpful*
muss ehrlich sein	*must be honest*
darf nie auf andere Freunde eifersüchtig sein	*may never be jealous of other friends*
muss viel Geduld haben	*must have lots of patience*
kann mit mir über alles reden	*can talk to me about everything*
hat die gleichen Interessen	*has the same interests*
sieht gut aus	*looks good*
Das ist für mich …	*That is … to me.*
(nicht) wichtig	*(not) important*
wichtiger	*more important*
am wichtigsten	*the most important*
Wir sind miteinander befreundet, weil …	*We are friends with each other because …*
wir die gleichen Interessen haben	*we have the same interests*
wir viel zusammen lachen	*we laugh a lot together*
wir über alles reden können	*we can talk about everything*
Wir haben uns (in der Grundschule) kennengelernt.	*We met at primary school.*
Wir sind seit (dem Sommer) ein Pärchen.	*We have been a couple since (the summer).*

Had a look ☐ **Nearly there** ☐ **Nailed it** ☐

Beziehungen	*Relationships*
Ich komme (nicht so) gut mit … aus.	*I (don't) get on (so) well with …*
Ich verstehe mich (nicht so gut) mit …	*I (don't) get on (so) well with …*
Ich kann ihn/sie nicht leiden!	*I can't stand him/her!*
Er/Sie geht mir auf die Nerven.	*He/She gets on my nerves.*
Unsere Beziehung ist (nicht so) gut, weil er/sie …	*Our relationship is (not so) good … because he/she is …*
toll / sympathisch / lieb	*great / nice / kind*
hilfsbereit / ehrlich / ärgerlich ist	*helpful / honest / annoying*
(zu) vorsichtig	*(too) careful*
(zu) nicht hilfsbereit	*(too) not helpful*
weil er/sie (viel / keine) Geduld hat	*because he/she has (a lot of / no) patience*
weil er/sie (immer / nie) Zeit für mich hat	*because he/she (always / never) has time for me*

21

Kapitel 3 Wörter

weil er/sie mich (nicht) unterstützt	because he/she supports me / doesn't support me	wahrscheinlich	probably
		vielleicht	perhaps
		nicht	not

Had a look ☐ Nearly there ☐ Nailed it ☐

Had a look ☐ Nearly there ☐ Nailed it ☐

Ich streite mich mit …	I argue with …
meinem Vater / ihm	my father / him
meiner Mutter / ihr	my mother / her
meinen Geschwistern / ihnen	my brothers and sisters / them
Wir streiten uns um …	We argue about …
den Computer	the computer
die Kleidung	clothes
das Handy	the mobile phone
Geld	money
Freunde	friends
Wir haben uns um … gestritten.	We argued about …
Er/Sie findet, …	He/She thinks …
Sie finden, …	They think …
ich verbringe zu viel Zeit mit dem Handy	I spend too much time on my mobile
ich verbringe zu viel Zeit am Computer	I spend too much time on the computer
ich mache nicht genug Hausaufgaben	I don't do enough homework
ich gebe zu viel Geld aus	I spend too much money
ich bin eifersüchtig auf (meinen Bruder / meine Schwester)	I'm jealous of (my brother / my sister)
Er/Sie mag meine Kleidung nicht.	He/She doesn't like my clothes.
Sie mögen meine Freunde nicht.	They don't like my friends.

Had a look ☐ Nearly there ☐ Nailed it ☐

Mein Wochenende
My weekend

Ich werde am Sonntag …	On Sunday I will …
Ich werde am Wochenende …	At the weekend I will …
Rad fahren	go cycling
spazieren gehen	go for a walk
ins Freibad gehen	go to the open-air pool
im Internet surfen	surf the internet
soziale Netzwerke nutzen	use social networks
Hausaufgaben machen	do homework
in die Kirche gehen	go to church
einkaufen gehen	go shopping
Zeit mit Familie / Freunden verbringen	spend time with family / friends
grillen	have a barbecue
Musik hören	listen to music
einen Film gucken	watch a film
fernsehen	watch TV
bestimmt	definitely

Vorbilder
Role models

(Gandhi) ist ein (großes) Vorbild für mich.	(Gandhi) is a (great) role model for me.
Ich habe kein (berühmtes) Vorbild.	I don't have a (famous) role model.
Ich finde das oberflächlich.	I find that superficial.
Er/Sie inspiriert mich.	He/She inspires me.
Ich bewundere ihn/sie.	I admire him/her.
Ich habe vor ihm/ihr viel Respekt.	I have a lot of respect for him/her.
Ich finde ihn/sie …	I find him/her …
beeindruckend	impressive
begabt	talented
Sie helfen mir in meinem Leben, weil …	They help me in my life, because …
sie Menschen in Not unterstützen	they support people in need
sie mir eine Art Orientierungshilfe geben	they give me direction in life
sie eine Inspiration für uns sind	they are an inspiration for us
Er/Sie hilft mir in meinem Leben, weil …	He/She helps me in my life, because …
er so ein toller Sportler ist	he's such a great sportsman
er vielen Leuten hilft … denn …	he helps many people … because …
er hat sich für soziale Probleme interessiert	he was interested in social problems
er hat in seinem Leben vielen Leuten geholfen	he helped many people in his life
er war immer gegen Gewalt	he was always against violence

Had a look ☐ Nearly there ☐ Nailed it ☐

Damals und heute
Then and now

Als ich ein Kind war, …	When I was a child …
Mit (zehn) Jahren …	At age (ten) …
Früher …	Before …
war das Leben ziemlich schwer	life was quite hard
war meine Mutter oft krank	my mother was often ill
musste ich immer zu Hause helfen	I always had to help at home
konnte ich nie Zeit mit Freunden verbringen	I could never spend time with my friends
durfte ich niemanden nach Hause einladen	I was never allowed to invite anybody to my house

durfte ich nicht alleine (zur Schule) gehen	I was not allowed to go (to school) on my own
konnte ich abends schwimmen	I could swim in the evenings
Das war so unfair!	That was so unfair!

Had a look ☐   **Nearly there** ☐   **Nailed it** ☐

Heutzutage muss ich viel weniger machen.	Nowadays I have to do a lot less.
Im Moment ist es besser.	At the moment it's better.
Ich darf mit meinen Freunden ...	I'm allowed to ... with my friends.
Ich muss um 21 Uhr nach Hause kommen.	I have to be home by 9 p.m.
Das ist ...	That is ...
zu früh	too early
ein bisschen zu viel	a bit too much
Ich will länger ausgehen.	I want to stay out later.
Ich habe keine Zeit mehr für ...	I no longer have any time for ...
Ich will eine bessere Balance finden.	I want to find a better balance.
Ich muss ...	I must ...
fleißig in der Schule lernen	study hard at school
gute Noten bekommen	get good grades
Ich habe viel Freiheit.	I have a lot of freedom.
Ich darf ...	I am allowed to ...
abends ausgehen	go out in the evenings
mein Handy so viel benutzen, wie ich will	use my mobile as much as I want
soziale Netzwerke nutzen	use social networks
Ich bin doch kein Kind mehr!	After all, I'm not a child any more!

Had a look ☐   **Nearly there** ☐   **Nailed it** ☐

Kapitel 3 Wörter

Extra words I should know for reading and listening activities

Positive Charaktereigenschaften	**Positive personal characteristics**
gesund	healthy
gesprächig	chatty
großzügig	generous
klug	clever
lebendig	lively
optimistisch	optimistic
schüchtern	shy
treu	faithful
unabhängig	independent
vernünftig	reasonable
verständnisvoll	understanding
zuverlässig	reliable
guter Laune sein	to be in a good mood

Had a look ☐ Nearly there ☐ Nailed it ☐

Negative Charaktereigenschaften	**Negative personal characteristics**
angeberisch	pretentious
dickköpfig	stubborn
egoistisch*	egotistic, selfish
eingebildet	conceited
gemein*	mean, nasty
humorlos	humourless
neidisch	envious
peinlich	embarrassing
pessimistisch	pessimistic
rechthaberisch	bossy
selbstsüchtig*	selfish
stur	stubborn
verdorben	spoilt
verrückt	mad, crazy
verwöhnt	spoilt
schlechter Laune sein	to be in a bad mood

Had a look ☐ Nearly there ☐ Nailed it ☐

Beziehungen	**Relationships**
single	single
ledig	unmarried
unverheiratet	unmarried
verliebt	in love
verlobt	engaged
verheiratet	married
getrennt	separated
geschieden	divorced
sich verloben	to get engaged
heiraten	to get married
sich trennen	to separate, to split up
sich scheiden lassen	to get divorced
der/die Verlobte	fiancé(e)
der/die Alleinerziehende	single parent
adoptiert	adopted

Had a look ☐ Nearly there ☐ Nailed it ☐

Familie	**Family**
das Familienmitglied(er)	family member
der/die Verwandte	relative
der (Ehe-)Mann	husband
die (Ehe-)Frau	wife
die Großeltern	grandparents
der Opa(s)	grandpa
die Oma(s)	grandma
das Enkelkind(er)	grandchild
der Halbbruder(-brüder)	half-brother
die Stiefschwester(n)	stepsister
der Zwilling(e)	twin
der Onkel(-)	uncle
die Tante(n)	aunt
der Cousin(s)	(male) cousin
die Cousine(n)	(female) cousin
die Jugendlichen	young people, adolescents
der/die Erwachsene	adult
erwachsen	adult
aufpassen auf	to look after, to care for

Had a look ☐ Nearly there ☐ Nailed it ☐

Aussehen	**Appearance**
der Schnurrbart(-bärte)	moustache
eine Glatze haben	to be bald
altmodisch	old-fashioned
gepflegt	smart, neat
hässlich	ugly
schick	smart, chic
die Klamotten	clothes
die Mode	fashion
der Ohrring(e)	earring
Ich habe meinen eigenen Stil.	I have my own style.

Had a look ☐ Nearly there ☐ Nailed it ☐

Freundschaften / Friendships

der Einfluss	influence
der Freundeskreis	circle of friends
die Kommunikation	communication
die Persönlichkeit	character, personality
die Priorität(en)	priority
der Streit(e)	argument
der Typ	guy, dude, bloke
die Unterstützung	support
sich auf sich selbst konzentrieren	to concentrate on yourself
gemeinsam	together
kompliziert	complicated
kommunizieren	to communicate
plaudern	to chat, to chatter
schwatzen	to chat, to chatter
etwas vorhaben	to have something planned
Wir mögen die gleichen Dinge.	We like the same things.

Had a look ☐ **Nearly there** ☐ **Nailed it** ☐

Probleme zu Hause / Problems at home

ausbleiben	to stay out
sich einmischen	to interfere
lösen	to solve, to resolve
die Lösung(en)	solution
die Strategie(n)	strategy
ein negatives Körperbild	a negative body image
der/die Prominente*	celebrity, VIP
Das hat eine negative Seite.	That has a negative side.

Had a look ☐ **Nearly there** ☐ **Nailed it** ☐

---

*Look for cognates and near-cognates when working out meanings of new words.

Treu looks very similar to 'true', which is a synonym for 'faithful'.

Optimistisch and *pessimistisch* should be easy to work out and can you see the link between *gemein* and 'mean', or *egoistisch* and 'selfish' (or 'egotistical')?

Have a look at *der/die Prominente*. This is a near-cognate, literally meaning 'prominent person', or 'celebrity/VIP'.

Kapitel 4 Wörter

Words I should know for speaking and writing activities

Zu Hause — At home
der Flur	hall
der Keller	cellar, basement
der Garten	garden
die Garage	garage
die Küche	kitchen
das Arbeitszimmer	study
das Badezimmer	bathroom
das Esszimmer	dining room
das Schlafzimmer	bedroom
das Wohnzimmer	sitting room
Ich wohne (seit vier Jahren) …	I have been living … (for four years)
in einer Kleinstadt	in a small town
in einer Großstadt	in a city
in der Stadtmitte	in the town centre
am Stadtrand	on the outskirts / in the suburbs
auf dem Land	in the countryside

Had a look ☐   Nearly there ☐   Nailed it ☐

das Einfamilienhaus	detached house
die Doppelhaushälfte	semi-detached house
das Reihenhaus	terraced house
das Hochhaus	high-rise building
der Wohnblock	block of flats
die 3-Zimmer-Wohnung	3-room flat
im zweiten Stock	on the second floor
im Untergeschoss	in the basement
im Erdgeschoss	on the ground floor
der Autostellplatz	parking space
der Dachboden	loft, attic
die Terrasse	terrace, patio

Had a look ☐   Nearly there ☐   Nailed it ☐

Essen und trinken — Eating and drinking
Es schmeckt …	It tastes …
lecker / köstlich / wunderbar	tasty / delicious / wonderful
würzig	spicy
ekelhaft / (un)appetitlich	disgusting / (un)appetising
geschmacklos	tasteless
scharf / sauer	hot, spicy / sour
salzig / fettig	salty / fatty
Ich esse (nicht) gern …	I (don't) like eating …
Ich esse lieber …	I prefer eating …
Ich esse am liebsten …	I like eating … best.
das Lieblingsessen	favourite meal
Ich bin Vegetarier(in).	I am vegetarian.
die Auswahl	choice, selection
auswählen	to choose
einkaufen	to buy, to shop
anklicken	to click on
vorbereiten	to prepare
eine leckere Spezialität aus …	a tasty speciality from …
das Frühstück	breakfast
das Mittagessen	lunch
das Abendbrot	dinner, evening meal
das Abendessen	dinner, evening meal
Das (Abendbrot) essen wir um …	We eat (dinner) at …

Had a look ☐   Nearly there ☐   Nailed it ☐

Zum Frühstück oder Abendessen — For breakfast or dinner
das Brot	bread
die Brotsorte	type of bread
das Brötchen	bread roll
die Butter	butter
der Käse	cheese
die Wurst	sausage
der Wurstaufschnitt	selection of sliced cold sausage
der Schinken	ham
das Ei (die Eier)	egg
das Spiegelei(er)	fried egg
der Lachs	salmon
die Marmelade	jam
der Honig	honey
der Pampelmusensaft	grapefruit juice
der Kräutertee	herbal tea
die Milch	milk
die fettarme Milch	skimmed milk
der Früchtetee	fruit tea
der Kaffee	coffee
der Saft	juice
das Glas Sekt	glass of champagne

Had a look ☐   Nearly there ☐   Nailed it ☐

Zum Mittag- oder Abendessen — For lunch or dinner
der Sauerbraten	dish of marinated braised beef
das Gulasch	goulash
der Spargel	asparagus
das Schnitzel	schnitzel, escalope
das Rindersteak	beef steak
die Gemüsesuppe	vegetable soup
die Hühnersuppe	chicken soup
die Pizza (Margherita)	pizza (margherita)
das Schweinefleisch	pork
das Lammfleisch	lamb
die Nudeln (pl)	pasta, noodles
mit Tomaten- / Fleischsoße	with tomato / meat sauce

Kapitel 4 Wörter

ein gemischter Salat	a mixed salad
die Suppe	soup
der Fisch	fish
(mit) Kartoffeln / Reis	(with) potatoes / rice
die Pommes (pl)	chips
die Currywurst	sausage with curry sauce
das Sauerkraut	sauerkraut
das Fertiggericht	ready meal
die Limonade	lemonade
das Mineralwasser	mineral water
die Kartoffelchips (pl)	crisps

Had a look ☐ Nearly there ☐ Nailed it ☐

Süßes und Nachspeisen — Sweets and desserts

die Nachspeise	dessert
das Eis	ice cream
das Gebäck	baked goods, pastries
das Mehl	flour
der Keks(e)	biscuit
die Torte(n)	gâteau
hausgemachte Torte(n)	home-made gâteau(x)
der Berliner	doughnut
der (Zucchini-)Kuchen	(courgette) cake
die Vanillesoße	vanilla sauce, custard
der Apfelstrudel	apple strudel
der Pflaumenkuchen	plum cake
mit Sahne	with cream

Had a look ☐ Nearly there ☐ Nailed it ☐

Obst und Gemüse — Fruit and vegetables

das Obst	fruit
das Gemüse	vegetables
die Ananas(–)	pineapple
der Apfel (Äpfel)	apple
die Banane(n)	banana
die Birne(n)	pear
die Erdbeere(n)	strawberry
die Himbeere(n)	raspberry
die Kirsche(n)	cherry
die Orange(n)	orange
der Pfirsich(e)	peach
die Traube(n)	grape
die Zitrone(n)	lemon
der Blumenkohl(e)	cauliflower
die Erbse(n)	pea
die Gurke(n)	cucumber
die Karotte(n)	carrot
der Knoblauch	garlic
der Kohl(e)	cabbage
die Paprika(s)	pepper
die Tomate(n)	tomato
die Zwiebel(n)	onion

Had a look ☐ Nearly there ☐ Nailed it ☐

Auf Austausch — On an exchange visit

Herzlich willkommen!	Welcome!
Wie geht's dir / Ihnen?	How are you?
Wie war die Reise?	How was the journey?
Wie bitte?	Pardon?
Ich verstehe nicht.	I don't understand.
Hast du (Hausschuhe) mitgebracht?	Have you brought (slippers)?
Können Sie bitte langsamer sprechen?	Can you speak more slowly, please?
Kannst du das bitte wiederholen?	Can you repeat that, please?
Hast du / Haben Sie Hunger?	Are you hungry?
Hast du / Haben Sie Durst?	Are you thirsty?
Hast du eine Frage an uns?	Do you have a question for us?
Was meinst du damit?	What do you mean?
Was bedeutet „Hausschuhe"?	What does 'Hausschuhe' mean?
Wie heißt „Wi-Fi-Code" auf Deutsch?	How do you say 'WiFi code' in German?
Was ist dein / Ihr „Wi-Fi-Code", bitte?	What is your 'WiFi code', please?

Had a look ☐ Nearly there ☐ Nailed it ☐

Man muss …	We must …
die Fahrräder unten im Keller abstellen	put the bikes in the cellar
die Treppen sauber halten	keep the stairs clean
den Müll ordentlich trennen	separate the rubbish neatly
in der Ruhezeit ruhig sein	be quiet during 'quiet time'
die Hausordnung	house rules
die Mittagsruhe	quiet time at midday
die Ruhezeit	quiet time
Man darf keine laute Musik spielen.	We are not allowed to play loud music.
Man darf kein Instrument üben.	We are not allowed to practise an instrument.
Man darf nicht mit dem Ball spielen.	We are not allowed to play ball games.
Man darf nie das Auto vor der Garage waschen.	We are never allowed to wash the car in front of the garage.
der Tagesablauf	Daily routine
an einem Schultag	on a school day
täglich	daily
während der Woche	during the week
am Abend / Nachmittag	in the evening / afternoon
zuerst	first of all
anschließend	afterwards
stundenlang	for hours
am Wochenende	at the weekend

Had a look ☐ Nearly there ☐ Nailed it ☐

Kapitel 4 Wörter

Soziale Netzwerke und Technologie	Social networks and technology
simsen	to text
eine SMS schicken / senden	to send a text
per Handy / Internet telefonieren	to call on a mobile / via the internet
soziale Netzwerke nutzen	to use social networks
online / im Internet chatten	to chat online
im Internet surfen	to surf online
Fotos hochladen	to upload photos
Musik herunterladen	to download music
sich mit Freunden unterhalten	to chat with friends
E-Mails schreiben	to write emails
Briefe tippen	to type letters
einen Kommentar schreiben	to write a comment

Had a look ☐ **Nearly there** ☐ **Nailed it** ☐

Vor- und Nachteile der Technologie	Advantages and disadvantages of technology
Ein großer Vorteil der Technologie ist, dass …	A big advantage of technology is that …
Der größte Vorteil ist, dass …	The biggest advantage is that …
Ein großer Nachteil ist, dass …	A big disadvantage is that …
Der größte Nachteil ist, dass …	The biggest disadvantage is that …
Das Gute daran ist, dass …	The good thing about it is that …
Das Beste daran ist, dass …	The best thing about it is that …
Schlecht daran ist, dass …	What's bad about it is that …
Es gibt mehr Vorteile als Nachteile.	There are more advantages than disadvantages.
einerseits …	on the one hand … on the other hand
andererseits	
auf der einen Seite	on the one hand
auf der anderen Seite	on the other hand
im Großen und Ganzen	by and large
Vor allem ist das positiv, weil …	Above all, that is positive because …
Das Internet kann zu Problemen führen.	The internet can lead to problems.

Had a look ☐ **Nearly there** ☐ **Nailed it** ☐

der Bildschirm	screen
der Desktop-PC	desktop computer / PC
die Digitalkamera	digital camera
der MP3-Player	MP3 player
der Musik-Streaming-Dienst	music streaming service
das Smart-TV	Smart TV
das Tablet	tablet
die Konsole	console
das Handy	mobile phone
die Kopfhörer (pl)	headphones
gefährlich	dangerous
kreativ	creative
praktisch	practical
privat	private
schädlich	harmful
sicher	safe
spannend	exciting
süchtig	addicted
teuer	expensive
überraschend	surprising

Had a look ☐ **Nearly there** ☐ **Nailed it** ☐

Kapitel 4 Wörter

Extra words I should know for reading and listening activities

Wo ich wohne	**Where I live**
die Eigentumswohnung(en)	owner-occupied flat
das Privatbad	private/ensuite bathroom
das Waschbecken	washbasin
der Schreibtisch	desk
die Etage(n)	floor, storey
das Gebäude(–)	building
der Bauernhof(–höfe)	farm
der/die Mitbewohner(in)	fellow occupant, house / flatmate
der Rasen	lawn
mieten	to rent
renoviert	renovated
nebenan	next door

Had a look ☐ Nearly there ☐ Nailed it ☐

Die Tagesroutine	**Daily routine**
Ich frühstücke.	I have breakfast.
Ich gehe ins Bett.	I go to bed.
Ich setze mich an den Computer.*	I sit down at the computer.
Ich amüsiere mich.	I enjoy myself.
Ich langweile mich.	I get bored.
Ich treffe mich mit Freunden.	I meet friends.
das Alltagsleben	daily life
im Freien spielen	to play in the open air
den Tisch decken	to lay the table

Had a look ☐ Nearly there ☐ Nailed it ☐

Essen und trinken	**Eating and drinking**
die Mahlzeit(en)	meal
die Geburtstagstorte	birthday cake
pikant	spicy
gedämpft	steamed
gedünstet	steamed
gekocht	boiled, cooked
hausgemacht	home-made
das Getränk(e)	drink
die Flasche(n)	bottle
das Glas (Gläser)	jar, glass
die Packung(en)	packet
die Scheibe(n)	slice
das Stück(e)	piece
die Tasse(n)	cup
die Schüssel(n)	bowl
das Messer(–)	knife
die Gabel(n)	fork

der Löffel(–)	spoon
der Teelöffel(–)	teaspoon
die Serviette(n)	napkin
die Platte(n)	platter
das Fertiggericht(e)	ready meal

Had a look ☐ Nearly there ☐ Nailed it ☐

Technologie	**Technology**
der Blickkontakt	eye contact
persönliche Daten (pl)	personal information
der Drucker(–)	printer
die Gefahr(en)	danger
das persönliche Gespräch(e)	face-to-face conversation
das Internet-Mobbing	cyberbullying
die Körpersprache	body language
die Maus (Mäuse)	mouse
das Risiko (Risiken)	risk
die Sicherheit	security
die Tastatur(en)	keyboard
die Verbindung(en)	connection
sich ausdrücken	to express oneself
in Kontakt bleiben	to stay in contact
brennen	to burn
drucken	to print
laden	to load
löschen	to erase, to delete
absaven	to save, to store
sichern	to save, to store
speichern	to save, to store
per Festnetz telefonieren	to phone via landline
tippen	to type

Had a look ☐ Nearly there ☐ Nailed it ☐

---

*Check which case is used with the verbs *sich setzen* and *sitzen* to ensure you interpret the correct meaning:

*Ich setze mich **an den** Computer.* (movement – accusative)

I **sit down** at the computer.

*Ich sitze **am** Computer.* (no movement – dative)

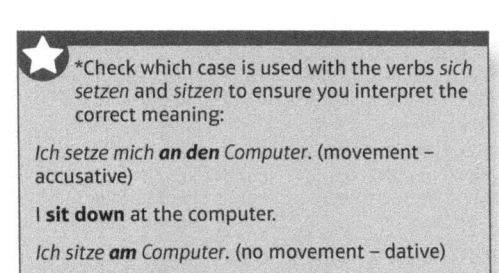

I **sit** at the computer.

29

Kapitel 5 Wörter

Words I should know for speaking and writing activities

Verkehrsmittel — Forms of transport
Ich fahre ... — I travel ...
mit dem Zug / Bus / Auto / Rad — by train / bus / car / bike
mit der U-Bahn / S-Bahn / Straßenbahn — by underground / urban railway / tram
Ich fliege mit dem Flugzeug. — I travel by plane.
Ich fliege. — I fly.
Ich gehe zu Fuß. — I go on foot. / I walk.

Had a look ☐ **Nearly there** ☐ **Nailed it** ☐

Hotelzimmer reservieren — Booking hotel rooms
Ich möchte ... reservieren. — I would like to reserve ...
ein Einzelzimmer — a single room
zwei Doppelzimmer — two double rooms
ein Zimmer mit Aussicht — a room with a view
für eine Nacht — for one night
für zwei Nächte vom 8. bis 10. November — for two nights from 8 to 10 November
Gibt es WLAN im Hotel? — Is there Wi-Fi in the hotel?
der Fitnessraum (–räume) — gym
der Parkplatz(–plätze) — car park, parking space
das Restaurant(s) — restaurant
Darf ich den Hund zum Hotel mitbringen? — Can I bring my dog with me to the hotel?
Um wie viel Uhr ist das Frühstück / Abendessen? — What time is breakfast / dinner?
Wie viel kostet das Zimmer? — How much is the room?

Had a look ☐ **Nearly there** ☐ **Nailed it** ☐

Fahrkarten kaufen — Buying train tickets
Ich möchte eine Fahrkarte nach Berlin, bitte. — I'd like a ticket to Berlin, please.
Einfach oder hin und zurück? — Single or return?
Wann fährt der nächste Zug ab? — When does the next train leave?
Er fährt um 12:51 Uhr vom Gleis 22 ab. — It leaves at 12:51 from platform 22.
Wann kommt er an? — When does it arrive?
Er kommt in Berlin um 19:18 Uhr an. — It arrives in Berlin at 19:18.
Fährt der Zug direkt oder muss ich umsteigen? — Does the train go direct or do I need to change?

Had a look ☐ **Nearly there** ☐ **Nailed it** ☐

Ferienunterkunft — Holiday accommodation
das Hotel(s) — hotel
das Gasthaus(–häuser) — guest house, bed and breakfast
die Ferienwohnung(en) — holiday apartment
die Jugendherberge(n) — youth hostel
der Campingplatz (–plätze) — campsite
Ich würde am liebsten (in diesem Hotel) übernachten. — I would like best to stay (in this hotel).
in der Stadtmitte / im Stadtzentrum — in the town centre
am Stadtrand — in the suburbs / outskirts
am nächsten (zum Bahnhof) — nearest (to the station)
(Der Bahnhof) liegt (100 m) entfernt. — (The station) is (100 m) away.

Had a look ☐ **Nearly there** ☐ **Nailed it** ☐

der Computerraum (–räume) — computer room
der Fernsehraum (–räume) — TV room
der Garten (Gärten) — garden
der Spieleraum(–räume) — games room
der Supermarkt (–märkte) — supermarket
der Waschsalon(s) — launderette
die Klimaanlage(n) — air conditioning
das Freibad(–bäder) mit Sauna(s) — open-air pool with sauna
Er/Sie/Es ist ... / sieht ... aus. — It is / looks ...
modern — modern
praktisch — practical / handy
ruhig — quiet
altmodisch — old-fashioned
chaotisch — chaotic
schmutzig — dirty
(un)bequem — (un)comfortable

Had a look ☐ **Nearly there** ☐ **Nailed it** ☐

Urlaubsbeschwerden — Holiday complaints
Das Zimmer war klein und schmutzig. — The room was small and dirty.
Es waren lange Haare in der Dusche / im Waschbecken. — There were long hairs in the shower / in the washbasin.
Ich war total unzufrieden. — I was totally dissatisfied.
Ich werde nie wieder in diesem Hotel übernachten. — I will never stay in this hotel again.
Dieses Gasthaus hatte keinen Internetanschluss. — This guest house had no internet connection.

Kapitel 5 Wörter

Es gab keine Klimaanlage.	There was no air conditioning.
Das Frühstück war ein Höhepunkt.	Breakfast was a highlight.
Es gab Renovierungsarbeiten.	There were renovation works.
Es gab viel Lärm.	There was a lot of noise.
Unser Zelt war direkt neben dem Spieleraum / Waschsalon.	Our tent was right next to the games room / launderette.
Jede Nacht haben wir den Fernseher / die Discomusik / die Waschmaschinen gehört.	Every night we heard the TV / disco music / the washing machines.

Had a look ☐ Nearly there ☐ Nailed it ☐

Wegbeschreibungen — Directions

Fahr / Fahren Sie ...	Go ... (using a vehicle)
Geh / Gehen Sie ...	Go ... (walking)
rechts / links / geradeaus	right / left / straight on
weiter bis zum/zur ...	further until ...
über ...	over ...
Nimm / Nehmen Sie ...	Take ...
die erste / zweite Straße links	the first / second road on the left
Bieg / Biegen Sie an der Ecke rechts ab.	Turn right at the corner.
Überquer / Überqueren Sie ...	Cross ...
die Ampel(n)	the traffic lights
den Platz (Plätze)	the square
die Brücke(n)	the bridge
die Donau	the Danube
die Kreuzung(en)	crossroads

Had a look ☐ Nearly there ☐ Nailed it ☐

das Rathaus(–häuser)	town hall
der Rathausplatz (–plätze)	town hall square
das Museum (Museen)	museum
die Oper(n)	opera house
Es ist hundert Meter entfernt.	It's one hundred metres away.
Es ist auf der rechten Seite.	It's on the right.
Kannst du / Können Sie ... mir sagen, wie ich zum / zur ... komme?	Can you ... tell me how to get to ...?
mir den Weg zum / zur ... zeigen?	show me the way to ...?
Ich habe mich verlaufen.	I'm lost.
Kannst du / Können Sie mir helfen?	Can you help me?
Entschuldige / Entschuldigen Sie.	Excuse me.
Wo ist der / die / das ...?	Where is the ...?

Had a look ☐ Nearly there ☐ Nailed it ☐

Die Speisekarte — Menu

die Vorspeise(n)	starter
die Hauptspeise(n)	main course
die Nachspeise(n)	dessert
die Beilage(n)	side dish
die Getränkekarte(n)	drinks menu
das Tagesgericht(e)	dish of the day
Bedienung inbegriffen	service included
gefüllt	filled, stuffed
gemischt	mixed
geröstet	roast
hausgemacht	home-made
das Bier vom Fass	draught beer
der Fruchtsaft	fruit juice
der Wein	wine

Had a look ☐ Nearly there ☐ Nailed it ☐

Im Restaurant — In the restaurant

Wir möchten einen Tisch ... haben.	We'd like a table ...
für (vier) Personen	for (four) people
mit Aussicht auf die Donau	with a view of the Danube
in der Ecke	in the corner
hier links	on the left here
Könnte ich bitte (die Speisekarte / Getränkekarte) haben?	Could I have (the menu / drinks menu), please?
Das Tagesgericht ist ...	The dish of the day is ...

Had a look ☐ Nearly there ☐ Nailed it ☐

Restaurantbeschwerden — Restaurant complaints

Ich möchte mich beschweren.	I would like to make a complaint!
Dieser Löffel ist schmutzig.	This spoon is dirty.
Es ist ein Haar in diesem Salat.	There's a hair in this salad.
Dieser Tisch ...	This table ...
ist sehr laut	is very noisy
hat keine Aussicht	has no view
ist in der dunkelsten Ecke	is in the darkest corner
Das Bier ist zu warm.	The beer is too warm.
Dieser Wurstteller war sehr fettig.	This sausage platter was very fatty.
Das war (die schrecklichste Suppe).	That was (the most terrible soup).
Ich konnte (das Tagesgericht) nicht essen, weil es ... war.	I couldn't eat (the dish of the day) because it was ...

Had a look ☐ Nearly there ☐ Nailed it ☐

Kapitel 5 Wörter

Souvenirs | Souvenirs
der Kuli(s)	ballpoint pen
der Schmuck	jewellery
die Brieftasche(n)	wallet
das Portemonnaie(s)	purse
die Tasse(n)	mug, cup
das Bild(er)	picture
das Kopfkissen(–)	pillow, cushion
das Tischtuch(–tücher)	table cloth
der Keks(e)	biscuit
bunt	multi-coloured
(grün-weiß) gestreift	(green and white) striped
preiswert	inexpensive, good value
weich	soft

Had a look ☐ Nearly there ☐ Nailed it ☐

Einkaufen | Shopping
der Markt (Märkte)	market
der Souvenirladen (–läden)	souvenir shop
das Kaufhaus(–häuser)	department store
das Einkaufszentrum (–zentren)	shopping centre
Ich suche (ein T-Shirt) als Geschenk für (meinen Bruder).	I'm looking for (a T-shirt) as a present for (my brother).
Welche Größe hat (er)?	What size is (he)?
klein / mittelgroß / groß	small / medium / large
Seine Lieblingsfarben sind ...	His favourite colours are ...
altmodisch	old-fashioned
beliebt	popular
kaputt	broken
kurz / lang	short / long
preiswert	inexpensive, good value
schmutzig	dirty
teuer	expensive
im Sonderangebot	on special offer
... funktioniert nicht	... doesn't work
... passt mir nicht	... doesn't fit me
... hat ein Loch	... has a hole

Had a look ☐ Nearly there ☐ Nailed it ☐

Ein Problem melden | Reporting a problem
Mir ist schlecht / kalt.	I feel ill / cold.
Das Bein tut mir weh.	My leg hurts.
Ich habe mir den Arm verletzt.	I have injured my arm.
Ich möchte einen Handy-Diebstahl melden.	I'd like to report a mobile phone theft.
(Meine Mutter) ist auf dem Bürgersteig gefallen.	(My mother) fell over on the pavement.
Ich möchte mich über (die Toiletten) beschweren.	I'd like to complain about (the toilets).
Ich suche einen Geldautomaten.	I'm looking for a cash point.
Ich habe (meine Schlüssel / meine Brieftasche) verloren.	I have lost (my keys / my wallet).
Ich habe meinen Rucksack (im Café) gelassen.	I left my rucksack (in the café).
Gibt es hier in der Nähe ein Fundbüro / eine Apotheke?	Is there a lost-property office / chemist near here?
Sie müssen / Du musst ...	You must ...
zur Polizeiwache gehen	go to the police station
zum Fundbüro gehen	go to the lost-property office
ins Krankenhaus gehen	go to hospital
das Formular ausfüllen	fill in the form
Ich werde es dem Manager sagen.	I will tell the manager.
Ich werde einen Krankenwagen rufen.	I will call an ambulance.

Had a look ☐ Nearly there ☐ Nailed it ☐

In der Apotheke | At the chemist's
Ich habe Kopfweh.	I have a headache.
Ich leide unter Migräne.	I suffer from migraines.
Ich habe Zahnschmerzen.	I have a toothache.
Ich habe mir den Arm verletzt.	I have injured my arm.
Ich bin müde / erschöpft.	I am tired / exhausted.
Ich habe Husten.	I have a cough.
Ich habe Halsschmerzen.	I have a sore throat.
Sie müssen / könnten ...	You must / could ...
Tabletten / Vitamine / Hustenbonbons nehmen	take tablets / vitamins / throat sweets
eine Salbe benutzen	use an ointment
beim Zahnarzt anrufen	call the dentist
einen Termin ausmachen	make an appointment
ins Krankenhaus gehen	go to hospital

Had a look ☐ Nearly there ☐ Nailed it ☐

Kapitel 5 Wörter

Extra words I should know for reading and listening activities

Unterwegs	**On the move**
der Bahnsteig(e)	platform
der Bürgersteig(e)	pavement
die Bushaltestelle(n)	bus stop
der Fahrkartenschalter(–)	ticket counter
das Fahrzeug(e)	vehicle
der Fußgänger(–)	pedestrian
der Fußgängerübergang (–gänge)	pedestrian crossing
der Kreisverkehr(–)	roundabout (traffic)
die Linie	line
das Mofa(s)	moped
das Motorrad(–räder)	motorbike
der Reisebus(–busse)	coach
die Route	route
die Umleitung(en)	diversion
der Wartesaal(-säle)	waiting room
der Wohnwagen(–)	caravan

Had a look ☐ Nearly there ☐ Nailed it ☐

Mit dem Zug fahren	**Travelling by train**
die Bahnkarte(n)	railcard
die Ermäßigung(en)	reduction
der Fahrplan(–pläne)	timetable
das Gepäck	luggage
die Seniorenkarte(n)	senior citizen card
die Verspätung(en)	delay
besetzt	occupied, taken (seat)
umweltfreundlich	environmentally friendly
einsteigen*	to get on (bus, train, etc.)
aussteigen*	to get off (bus, train, etc.)

Had a look ☐ Nearly there ☐ Nailed it ☐

Unterkunft	**Accommodation**
die Pension(en)	bed and breakfast
die Halbpension	half board
die Vollpension	full board
das Lokal(e)	pub
das Hotelpersonal	hotel staff
der Empfangschef/die Empfangsdame	receptionist
der Aufenthaltsraum (–räume)	common room, lounge

der Aufzug(–züge)	lift
der Fahrstuhl(–stühle)	lift
das Zweibettzimmer	twin room
die Reservierung(en)	reservation
die Anmeldung	registration, booking in
der Aufenthalt	stay
der Rabatt(e)	discount

Had a look ☐ Nearly there ☐ Nailed it ☐

Beschwerden	**Complaints**
die Bettwäsche	bed linen
der Schlafsack(–säcke)	sleeping bag
die Heizung	heating
der Koffer(–)	suitcase
sich beklagen	to complain
sich beschweren	to complain
bemängeln	to find fault with
zelten	to camp
bestätigen	to confirm
ungenügend	unsatisfactory
im Voraus	in advance

Had a look ☐ Nearly there ☐ Nailed it ☐

Rund um die Stadt	**Around town**
der Alptraum	nightmare
der Ausgang(–gänge)	exit
der Besucher(–)	visitor
der Eingang(–gänge)	entrance
der Eintritt	entry, admission (to place / event)
die Eintrittskarte(n)	entry / admission ticket
die Kneipe	pub
das Nachtleben	nightlife
die Öffnungszeiten	opening times
die Richtung	direction
die Rundfahrt(en)	tour (on transport)
der Rundgang(–gänge)	tour (walking)
der Schnellimbiss(e)	snack (bar)
der Stadtplan(–pläne)	town plan, map
der Unfall	accident
das Verkehrsamt	tourist information office
sehenswert	worth seeing
sich verlaufen**	to get lost

Had a look ☐ Nearly there ☐ Nailed it ☐

---

*Look carefully at small words at the start of verbs which can change their meaning:

einsteigen to get in/on   Ich **steige** in den Bus **ein**.
aussteigen to get out/off Er **steigt** aus dem Zug **aus**.
umsteigen   to change   Wir **steigen** in Köln **um**.
(e.g. trains)

**'To get lost' in German is *sich verlaufen*. Don't fall into the trap of using the verb *verlieren*.

Ich habe mich in der Stadtmitte verlaufen.
I got lost in the town centre.

Words I should know for speaking and writing activities

Länder und Orte	Countries and places
im Ausland	abroad
Bayern	Bavaria
die Ostsee	the Baltic Sea
die Nordsee	the North Sea
Spanien	Spain
Italien	Italy
die Türkei	Turkey
Österreich	Austria
Kroatien	Croatia
Frankreich	France
die Schweiz	Switzerland
Großbritannien	Great Britain
Griechenland	Greece
Ich fahre / reise / fliege …	I go / travel / fly …
nach Deutschland	to Germany
in die Türkei	to Turkey
an einen See	to a lake
an das (ans) Meer	to the sea
an den Strand	to the beach / seaside
an die Küste	to the coast
auf eine Insel	to an island
in den Wald	to the forest / woods
in die Berge	to the mountains

Had a look ☐ Nearly there ☐ Nailed it ☐

Himmelsrichtungen	Points of the compass
der Kompass	compass
der Norden	north
der Nordosten	north east
der Osten	east
der Südosten	south east
der Süden	south
der Südwesten	south west
der Westen	west
der Nordwesten	north west
in der Mitte	in the middle

Had a look ☐ Nearly there ☐ Nailed it ☐

Das Wetter	The weather
Es ist …	It is …
heiß	hot
kalt	cold
sonnig	sunny
trocken	dry
regnerisch	rainy
windig	windy
wolkig	cloudy
neblig	foggy
frostig	frosty
stürmisch	stormy
wechselhaft	changeable

Es …	It's …
friert	freezing
hagelt	hailing
regnet	raining
schneit	snowing

Had a look ☐ Nearly there ☐ Nailed it ☐

Es gibt …	There is (are) …
Nebel	fog
Regen(–schauer)	rain (showers)
einen Sturm	a storm
ein Gewitter	a thunderstorm
Die Temperaturen liegen zwischen (15) und (18) Grad.	Temperatures lie between (15) and (18) degrees.
Die Temperatur ist hoch / niedrig.	The temperature is high / low.
Es wird windig / neblig sein.	It will be windy / foggy.
Es wird frieren / regnen / schneien.	It will freeze / rain / snow.
Es wird … geben.	There will be …
(keinen) Regen	(no) rain
(keine) Wolken	(no) clouds

Had a look ☐ Nearly there ☐ Nailed it ☐

Die Jahreszeiten	The seasons
der Frühling / das Frühjahr	spring
der Sommer	summer
der Herbst	autumn
der Winter	winter

Had a look ☐ Nearly there ☐ Nailed it ☐

Urlaubsarten	Types of holidays
Ich mache (nicht) gern …	I (don't) like …
Pauschalurlaub	a package holiday
Aktivurlaub	an active holiday
Erlebnisurlaub	an adventure holiday
Strandurlaub	a beach holiday
Winterurlaub	a winter holiday
Sightseeingurlaub	a sightseeing holiday
Urlaub auf Balkonien	a staycation, a holiday at home
Ich gehe (nicht) gern zelten, weil ich …	I (don't) like going camping because I …
abenteuerlustig bin	am adventurous
gern draußen bin	like being outdoors
gern in der Sonne liege	like sunbathing
gern andere Kulturen erlebe	like experiencing other cultures
mich für die Natur interessiere	am interested in nature

Kapitel 6 Wörter

mich entspannen will	want to relax
mich schnell langweile	get bored easily
nichts tun will	don't want to do anything

Had a look ☐   Nearly there ☐   Nailed it ☐

Wie war der Urlaub? — How was the holiday?

Die Reise ...	The journey ...
war furchtbar	was awful
hat ewig gedauert	lasted forever
Wir mussten stundenlang im Auto sitzen.	We had to sit in the car for hours.
Es gab einen Stau auf der Autobahn.	There was a traffic jam on the motorway.
Wir haben uns die ganze Zeit gestritten.	We argued / quarrelled the whole time.
Der Zug hatte Verspätung.	The train was delayed.
Das Bad war dreckig.	The bath was dirty.
Die Dusche hat nicht funktioniert.	The shower didn't work.
Die Ferienwohnung war ...	The holiday apartment was ...
gut eingerichtet	well-furnished
sehr sauber	very clean

Had a look ☐   Nearly there ☐   Nailed it ☐

Während des Urlaubs ...	During the holiday ...
sind wir in den Bergen wandern gegangen	we went walking in the mountains
war das Wetter wunderschön	the weather was beautiful
hat es jeden Tag geregnet	it rained every day
Wir haben den Urlaub genossen.	We enjoyed the holiday.
Die Landschaft war sehr schön.	The scenery was very beautiful.
Das Essen hat mir sehr gut geschmeckt.	I really liked the food.
außerhalb	outside of
innerhalb	inside, within
statt	instead of
trotz	in spite of
während	during
wegen	because of

Had a look ☐   Nearly there ☐   Nailed it ☐

Eine Feier organisieren — Organising a party

Mein Freund hatte mich zur Party in ... eingeladen.	My friend had invited me to the party in ...
Ich hatte ... organisiert.	I had organised ...
den Urlaub	the holiday
die Feier	the party
das Wochenende	the weekend
Meine Freunde hatten ... gekauft.	My friends had bought ...
das Essen / die Getränke / Luftballons	the food / the drinks / balloons
Wir haben (gefeiert / getanzt / gegessen).	We (celebrated / danced / ate).
Ich war (zum Bahnhof) gefahren.	I had gone (to the station).
Ich hatte (mein Handy) vergessen.	I had forgotten (my mobile phone).

Had a look ☐   Nearly there ☐   Nailed it ☐

Urlaubsartikel — Holiday items

das Visum	visa
die Buchungsbestätigung	booking confirmation
der Reisepass	passport
die Medikamente	medicines
der Führerschein	driving licence
der Jugendherbergsausweis	youth hostel membership card
die Reise-Apps	travel apps
der Personalausweis	identity card

Had a look ☐   Nearly there ☐   Nailed it ☐

Absichten äußern — Expressing intentions

planen	to plan
hoffen	to hope
Lust haben	to be keen
vorhaben	to intend
um ... zu	in order to
ohne ... zu	without

Had a look ☐   Nearly there ☐   Nailed it ☐

Wenn ... — If ...

Wenn ich mehr Geld / mehr Zeit / keine (Flug-) Angst hätte, ...	If I had more money / more time / no fear (of flying), ...
Wenn ich mutiger / reicher wäre, ... würde ich ...	If I were braver / richer ... I would ...
nach Australien / zum Mond fliegen	fly to Australia / to the moon
auf Safari gehen	go on safari
in einem Luxushotel übernachten	stay in a luxury hotel

Had a look ☐   Nearly there ☐   Nailed it ☐

Wo ich wohne — Where I live

Es gibt einen Flughafen / Bahnhof.	There is an airport / a station.
Es gab keine Autobahn / Schule / Universität.	There was no motorway / school / university.

K6

35

Kapitel 6 Wörter

Es wird ... geben.	There will be ...
ein Fußballstadion / Kino	a football stadium / cinema
Fußgängerzonen / Touristen	pedestrian precincts / tourists
Leuchttürme / Museen	lighthouses / museums
nicht so viele Autos	not so many cars

Had a look ☐   Nearly there ☐   Nailed it ☐

Meine Stadt: Vor- und Nachteile
My town: advantages and disadvantages

Ich wohne in einer Stadt / in einem Vorort, wo ...	I live in a town / suburb where ...
man (Lebensmittel) kaufen kann	you can buy (groceries)
es (eine Bäckerei) gibt	there's a (bakery)
ich überall zu Fuß hinkomme	I can get everywhere on foot
ich mich nie langweile	I never get bored
es oft zu laut ist	it is often too noisy
es zu viel Verkehr / Müll gibt	there is too much traffic / rubbish
Es gibt in der Umgebung ...	In the neighbourhood there is ...
fast nichts für junge Leute	virtually nothing for young people
ein vielseitiges Kulturangebot	a varied cultural offering

Had a look ☐   Nearly there ☐   Nailed it ☐

Wir haben früher ... gewohnt.	Before, we lived ...
in einer Kleinstadt / Großstadt	in a small town / city
außerhalb der Stadt	outside the town
Es gab weder Freibad noch Tennisplatz.	There was neither an open-air pool nor a tennis court.
Man sollte / könnte ...	We should / could ...
vielseitige Aktivitäten für Jugendliche anbieten	offer varied activities for young people
neue Parkplätze am Stadtrand bauen	build new car parks on the outskirts of the town
die öffentlichen Verkehrsmittel verbessern	improve public transport
mehr Wohnungen bauen	build more flats
mehr Fahrradwege haben	have more cycle paths
Autos in der Innenstadt verbieten, um Staus zu reduzieren	ban cars from the town centre to reduce traffic jams
die Straßen sauber halten	keep the streets clean

Had a look ☐   Nearly there ☐   Nailed it ☐

Kapitel 6 Wörter

Extra words I should know for reading and listening activities

Urlaubsplanung	*Planning holidays*
das Boot(e)	boat
die Fähre(n)	ferry
die Seilbahn(en)	cable car
das Wohnmobil(e)*	camper van
die Vorbereitung(en)	preparation
die Landkarte(n)	map
der Abstecher(–)	detour
die Hauptsaison	high season
inklusive	included
im Angebot	on offer
bezahlbar	affordable
vorher	before(hand)
bieten	to offer
buchen	to book
zur Verfügung stehen	to be available

Had a look ☐ **Nearly there** ☐ **Nailed it** ☐

Meine Gegend	*My area*
die Aufregung	excitement
das Gebiet(e)	area
die Geschwindigkeit	speed
die Geschwindigkeits-begrenzung	speed limit
die Grünanlage(n)	green space, park
die Industrie(n)	industry
die Landwirtschaft	agriculture
der Lastwagen(–)	lorry
die Raststätte(n)	motorway services
der Stadtteil(e)	part of town
das Stadtviertel(–)	district, quarter (of a town)
die Stoßzeit	rush hour
der Vorort(e)	suburb

Had a look ☐ **Nearly there** ☐ **Nailed it** ☐

Im Urlaub	*On holiday*
baden	to swim, to bathe
die Ausstellung(en)	exhibition
die Autovermietung	car hire
der Badeort(e)*	seaside resort, spa
die Eishalle(n)	ice rink
der Fahrradverleih	bike hire
das Festland	mainland
der Hafen (Häfen)	port
der Laden (Läden)	shop
die Lage(n)	situation, position
der Spielplatz(–plätze)	playground
die Sportanlagen (pl)	sports facilities
das Tal (Täler)	valley
der Tourismus	tourism
die Unterhaltungs-möglichkeiten	entertainment opportunities, things to do
die Veranstaltung(en)	event
einen Sonnenbrand bekommen	to get sunburnt
erholsam	restful
Schlittschuh laufen	to go ice skating
entdecken	to discover

Had a look ☐ **Nearly there** ☐ **Nailed it** ☐

Das Wetter	*The weather*
das Klima	climate
die Wettervorhersage	weather forecast
die Höchsttemperatur	highest temperature
die Tiefsttemperatur	lowest temperature
die Durchschnitts-temperatur	average temperature
steigen	to rise (temperature)
heiter	bright
bedeckt	overcast
aufklären	to brighten up
die Aufheiterung(en)	bright spell
der Niederschlag	precipitation, rainfall

Had a look ☐ **Nearly there** ☐ **Nailed it** ☐

> ⭐ *To work out the meaning of a new word, ask yourself if it is similar to one you already know, and if it contains cognates or near-cognates:*
>
> *das Wohnmobil* → *wohnen* (to live) + *mobil* (mobile) = 'mobile home', or 'camper van'
>
> *der Badeort* → *baden* (to swim / bathe) + *Ort* (place) = 'swimming place' or 'seaside resort'
>
> Remember to think beyond the literal translation when working out the correct English meaning.

K6

Words I should know for speaking and writing activities

Berufe — Jobs

der/die Anwalt/Anwältin	lawyer
der/die Apotheker(in)	chemist
der/die Architekt(in)	architect
der/die Arzt/Ärztin	doctor
der/die Bäcker(in)	baker
der/die Bankangestellte	bank clerk
der/die Beamte/Beamtin	civil servant
der/die Bibliothekar(in)	librarian
der/die Chef(in)	boss
der/die Dolmetscher(in)	interpreter
der/die Elektriker(in)	electrician
der/die Feuerwehrmann/-frau	firefighter
der/die Friseur/Friseuse	hairdresser
der/die Informatiker(in)	computer scientist
der/die Journalist(in)	journalist
der/die Kellner(in)	waiter/waitress
der/die Klempner(in)	plumber

Had a look ☐ Nearly there ☐ Nailed it ☐

der/die Koch/Köchin	cook
der/die Kraftfahrer(in)	lorry driver
der/die Krankenpfleger/Krankenschwester	nurse
der/die Lehrer(in)	teacher
der/die Manager(in)	manager
der/die Mechaniker(in)	mechanic
der/die Metzger(in)	butcher
der/die Pilot(in)	pilot
der/die Polizist(in)	police officer
der/die Programmierer(in)	computer programmer
der/die Schauspieler(in)	actor/actress
der/die Sozialarbeiter(in)	social worker
der/die Tierarzt/Tierärztin	vet
der/die Verkäufer(in)	sales assistant
der/die Steward(ess)	air steward(ess)
der/die Übersetzer(in)	translator

Had a look ☐ Nearly there ☐ Nailed it ☐

Arbeitsorte — Places of work

der Keller(-)	cellar
der Laden (Läden)	shop
die Apotheke(n)	chemist's
die Autowerkstatt (-stätten)	garage
die Bäckerei(en)	bakery
die Bank(en)	bank
die Metzgerei(en)	butcher's
die Polizeiwache(n)	police station
das Büro(s)	office
das Flugzeug(e)	aeroplane
das Geschäft(e)	shop
das Krankenhaus (-häuser)	hospital
das Labor(s)	laboratory
das Reisebüro(s)	travel agency
das Restaurant(s)	restaurant
das Theater(-)	theatre

Had a look ☐ Nearly there ☐ Nailed it ☐

Ein Praktikum — A work experience

Beim Arbeitspraktikum musste ich …	For my work experience I had to …
Glücklicherweise musste ich keine …	Fortunately I didn't have to …
Telefonanrufe machen	make phone calls
Akten / Dokumente abheften	file files / documents
Formulare ausfüllen	fill in forms
E-Mails schreiben	write emails
Gäste bedienen	serve customers
Autos waschen	wash cars
Termine organisieren	organise meetings
Ich musste auch (keinen) …	I also did (not) have to …
Tee / Kaffee machen	make tea / coffee

Had a look ☐ Nearly there ☐ Nailed it ☐

Berufsbilder — Job descriptions

Sie haben ausgezeichnete … Deutschkenntnisse	You have an excellent … knowledge of German
Sprachkenntnisse	knowledge of languages
Sie sind in (Deutsch) fließend.	You are fluent in (German).
Sie müssen hervorragende Kommunikationsfähigkeiten haben.	You need to have excellent communication skills.
Sie sind für die technischen Aspekte verantwortlich.	You are responsible for the technical aspects.
Sie beschäftigen sich mit (Strom).	You deal with (electricity).
Sie …	You …
schreiben Reportagen	write reports
decken Skandale auf	uncover scandals
berichten über viele aktuelle Themen	report on lots of current issues
interviewen (die Stars)	interview (the stars)
Sie müssen …	You must …
zuverlässig sein	be reliable

Kapitel 7 Wörter

Ihre Arbeit pünktlich abliefern	deliver your work on time	gehe ich zur Musikgruppe	I have been going to a music group
Sie brauchen eine gute Ausbildung.	You need a good education.	Ich besuche einen (Computer-)Kurs.	I attend a (computer) course.
		Ich habe einen (Textverarbeitungs-)Kurs besucht.	I attended a (word-processing) course.

Had a look ☐ **Nearly there** ☐ **Nailed it** ☐

Ein Hochschulabschluss / Arbeitserfahrung ist nicht notwendig.	A degree / Work experience is not necessary.
Wenn Sie einen Hochschulabschluss machen, verdienen Sie schneller ein höheres Gehalt.	If you graduate, you earn a higher salary more quickly.
Ihr Gehalt ist niedrig / großzügig / ausgezeichnet.	Your salary is low / generous / excellent.
Die Arbeitsbedingungen sind besonders gut / schlecht.	The working conditions are particularly good / bad.
Es gibt gute / wenige Aufstiegsmöglichkeiten.	There are good / few opportunities for promotion.
Sie arbeiten ...	You work ...
auf Baustellen	on building sites
bei einer Firma	for a company
freiberuflich von zu Hause aus	freelance from home
in einem Geschäft	in a shop
in einem Altenheim	in a care home for older people
in einem Krankenhaus	in a hospital
zuerst	first(ly)
danach	after that
dann	then
anschließend	finally

Had a look ☐ **Nearly there** ☐ **Nailed it** ☐

Bewerbungen — *Applications*

Ich interessiere mich für den Job als ..., weil ...	I'm interested in the job as ... because ...
ich (in Mathe) begabt bin	I'm good at / gifted in (maths)
ich (in der Touristik) arbeiten möchte	I would like to work in (tourism)
ich verantwortungsbewusst bin	I'm responsible
ich selbstständig sein will	I want to be independent
Seit drei Jahren ...	For three years ...
bin ich Mitglied im Orchester	I have been a member of an orchestra
bin ich Kapitän der (Handball-)Mannschaft	I have been captain of the (handball) team
gehe ich zum Sportverein	I have been going to a sports club

Ich bekomme gute Noten.	I get good grades.
Meine Noten sind nicht so gut.	My grades are not so good.
Meine Durchschnittsnote ist ...	My average grade is ...
Ich habe einen Teilzeitjob als (Touristenführer(in)).	I have a part-time job as a (tour guide).
Letzten Sommer habe ich als (Freiwillige(r)) gearbeitet.	Last summer I worked as a (volunteer).
Ich bin ...	I am ...
kreativ	creative
musikalisch	musical
geduldig	patient
fleißig	hard-working
pünktlich	punctual

Had a look ☐ **Nearly there** ☐ **Nailed it** ☐

Mein Lebenslauf — *My CV*

die Schulbildung	school education
der Schulabschluss	school-leaving qualification
die Schulleistung	school achievement
die freiwillige Arbeit	voluntary work
der Hochschulabschluss	degree
die Berufserfahrung	professional experience
die Freizeitaktivitäten	leisure activities

Had a look ☐ **Nearly there** ☐ **Nailed it** ☐

Traumberufe — *Dream jobs*

Als Kind wollte ich (Clown / Feuerwehrmann) werden.	As a child, I wanted to be a (clown / firefighter).
Ich möchte ... arbeiten.	I would like to work ...
als (Manager(in))	as a (manager)
im Ausland	abroad
in (den USA)	in (the USA)
freiwillig	voluntarily
in einem Elefantenheim	in an elephant home / elephant sanctuary
bei der Europäischen Kommission	for the European Commission

K 7

39

Kapitel 7 Wörter

bei einer (internationalen) Firma	for an (international) company
beim Zirkus	for a circus
Ich würde gern ...	I would like ...
in einer Hütte in den Alpen wohnen	to live in a hut / a cabin in the Alps
nach (Thailand) reisen	to travel to (Thailand)
ein Jahr in (Thailand) verbringen	to spend a year in (Thailand)
eine Lehre machen	to do an apprenticeship
Marketing machen	to do marketing

Had a look ☐   Nearly there ☐   Nailed it ☐

Sprachen öffnen Türen
Languages open doors

Im Moment lerne ich (Spanisch), um ...	At the moment I'm learning (Spanish) in order to ...
mich um einen guten Job zu bewerben	apply for a good job
die Leute / die Kultur / die Landessprache besser kennenzulernen	get to know the people / the culture / the national language better
nach (Spanien) auszuwandern	emigrate to (Spain)
Ich lerne (Deutsch), um ...	I'm learning (German) in order to ...
(an der Börse) zu arbeiten	work (at the stock exchange)
meine (Deutsch-) Kenntnisse zu verbessern	improve my knowledge (of German)
(die Liedertexte / Opern) richtig zu verstehen	understand (the lyrics / operas) properly
Ich möchte (Griechisch) lernen, um ...	I would like to learn (Greek) in order to ...
durch das Land zu reisen	travel around the country
mit Leuten in ihrer Muttersprache zu kommunizieren	communicate with people in their native language
mich zu amüsieren	have fun
Im Moment lerne ich (Mandarin), weil es ... ist.	At the moment I'm learning (Mandarin) because it's ...
ein Pflichtfach	a compulsory subject
nötig	necessary, essential
mir wichtig	important to me

Had a look ☐   Nearly there ☐   Nailed it ☐

Sprachen bei der Arbeit
Languages at work

Ich möchte etwas ... machen.	I would like to do something ...
Er/Sie würde gern etwas ... machen.	He/She would like to do something ...
ganz Anderes	completely different
Sinnvolles	meaningful
Aufregendes	exciting
Interessantes	interesting
Praktisches	practical
Neues	new
Ich möchte ...	I would like to ...
mich um eine Lehre / ein Praktikum als ... bewerben	apply for an apprenticeship / a work-experience placement as ...
in (der Autoindustrie) arbeiten	work in (the car industry)
bei (BMW) arbeiten	work for (BMW)
eine Bustour durch (Amerika) machen	go on a bus tour through (America)
(Fremdsprachen) an der Uni studieren	study (foreign languages) at university
Arbeitserfahrung sammeln	accumulate work experience
als Lehrling arbeiten	work as an apprentice / trainee
als ehrenamtlicher Mitarbeiter / ehrenamtliche Mitarbeiterin arbeiten	work as a volunteer

Had a look ☐   Nearly there ☐   Nailed it ☐

Kapitel 7 Wörter

Extra words I should know for reading and listening activities

Berufe	*Jobs*
der/die Angestellte	*employee*
der/die Arbeitgeber(in)	*employer*
der/die Bauarbeiter(in)*	*builder*
der/die Bauer/Bäuerin*	*farmer*
der/die Ingenieur(in)	*engineer*
der/die Kassierer(in)	*cashier*
der/die Kollege/Kollegin	*colleague*
der/die Sprachassistent(in)	*language assistant*
der/die Sprachliebhaber(in)	*language lover*
der/die Touristenführer(in)	*tourist guide*
der/die Vertreter(in)	*representative, sales rep*

Had a look ☐ **Nearly there** ☐ **Nailed it** ☐

Bei der Arbeit	*At work*
der Arbeitsplatz (-plätze)	*workplace*
die Besprechung(en)	*meeting*
die Gesellschaft(en)	*company, society*
die Kinderkrippe(n)	*crèche*
die Klinik(en)	*clinic*
die Konferenz(en)	*conference*
die Nachhilfe	*private tuition*
die Schichtarbeit	*shift work*
die Stelle(n)	*job*
der Termin(e)	*appointment*
die Touristik	*tourism*
das Treffen(-)	*meeting*

Had a look ☐ **Nearly there** ☐ **Nailed it** ☐

Bewerbungen	*Applications*
die Anzeige(n)	*advertisement*
der Bewerbungsbrief(e)	*letter of application*
das Bewerbungsformular(e)	*application form*
der Ehrgeiz	*ambition*
der Eindruck (Eindrücke)	*impression*
die Fähigkeit(en)	*skill, ability*
der Lohn	*wage*
die Möglichkeit(en)	*possibility*
die Notwendigkeit(en)	*necessity*
der Rat	*advice*
das Stellenangebot(e)	*job offer, situations vacant*
das Vorstellungs-gespräch(e)	*interview*
das Ziel(e)	*aim, goal*
die Zukunftspläne (pl)	*plans for the future*

Had a look ☐ **Nearly there** ☐ **Nailed it** ☐

ausgebildet	*qualified*
beilegen	*to enclose, to attach*
benötigen	*to need*
erfahren	*experienced*
sich konzentrieren	*to concentrate*
sich vorstellen	*to introduce oneself*
absolvieren	*to complete (course), to pass (exam)*
Jura	*law (subject)*
Medizin	*medicine (subject)*
das Semester(-)	*semester*
abwechslungsreich	*varied*
lehrreich	*educational*
das Familienleben	*family life*
der Lebensstil	*lifestyle*

Had a look ☐ **Nearly there** ☐ **Nailed it** ☐

---

*Look out for word families when working out the meaning of words, but remember to use the context of the text to help you too.

Bauen means 'to build' and *anbauen* means 'to grow' and you have come across several words using the stem *bau*:

Der Bauer and *der Bauarbeiter* both look similar, but one means 'farmer' and the other 'builder'.

Der Bauernhof and *die Baustelle* also look quite similar, but which is a 'farm', and which a 'building site'?

Using the language around the words will help you work out the meaning:

Ich wohne auf einem Bauernhof auf dem Land.

I live on a farm in the countryside.

Here, the verb *wohne* and the location *auf dem Land* help you decide that *Bauernhof* must be a farm rather than a building site.

41

Kapitel 8 Wörter

Words I should know for speaking and writing activities

Festivals und Events	Festivals and events
Letzten Sommer / Mai ...	Last summer / May ...
Letztes Jahr / Wochenende ...	Last year / weekend ...
habe ich das (Festival) gesehen	I saw the (festival)
bin ich zum (Event) gefahren	I went to the (event)
Ich habe dort ...	I ... there.
Fußball / Saxofon gespielt	played football / saxophone
nette Leute kennengelernt	met nice people
die Sehenswürdigkeiten besichtigt	visited the sights
die Spiele / die Bands gesehen	saw the games / bands
Das Konzert / Turnier hat in ... stattgefunden.	The concert / tournament took place in ...
Deutschland / England / Australien	Germany / England / Australia
Ich bin im Meer geschwommen.	I swam in the sea.
Das Festival war / fand ich ...	The festival was / I found the festival ...
etwas langweilig	a bit boring
sehr lustig	very funny
total spannend / super / toll	totally exciting / super / great
ziemlich laut	quite loud

Had a look ☐ **Nearly there** ☐ **Nailed it** ☐

Ein sportliches Event	A sporting event
der Streckenposten(–)	checkpoint
der Informationskiosk(e)	information stand
der Führungswagen(–)	lead car
die Ziellinie(n)	finish line
das Souvenirgeschäft(e)	souvenir shop
der Massageraum (–räume)	massage room
die Kleiderabgabe	cloakroom
die Kinderkrippe(n)	crèche

Had a look ☐ **Nearly there** ☐ **Nailed it** ☐

Die Olympischen Winterspiele

The Winter Olympics

(1976) fanden die Olympischen Spiele in (Innsbruck) statt.
(1.200) Sportler aus (37) Ländern haben teilgenommen.

(In 1976) the Olympic Games took place in (Innsbruck).
(1,200) sportspeople from (37) countries took part.

Es gab Wettbewerbe in (6) Sportarten.
Ein Vorteil ist / war ...
Ein Nachteil ist / war ...

There were competitions in (6) sports.
An advantage is / was ...
A disadvantage is / was ...

die Baustelle(n)	building site / construction site
die Gastgeberstadt (–städte)	host city
die Lärmbelastung	noise pollution
die Luftverschmutzung	air pollution
der Stau(s)	traffic jam
der Tourist(en)	tourist
der Zeitdruck	time pressure

Had a look ☐ **Nearly there** ☐ **Nailed it** ☐

Die Länder	Countries
Albanien	Albania
Armenien	Armenia
Australien	Australia
Belgien	Belgium
Deutschland	Germany
England	England
Estland	Estonia
Frankreich	France
Georgien	Georgia
Griechenland	Greece
Großbritannien	Great Britain
Israel	Israel
Italien	Italy
Kanada	Canada
Lettland	Latvia

Had a look ☐ **Nearly there** ☐ **Nailed it** ☐

Litauen	Lithuania
Montenegro	Montenegro
die Niederlande	the Netherlands
Norwegen	Norway
Österreich	Austria
Polen	Poland
Rumänien	Romania
Russland	Russia
Schweden	Sweden
die Schweiz	Switzerland
Serbien	Serbia
Slowenien	Slovenia
Spanien	Spain
Ungarn	Hungary
Zypern	Cyprus

Had a look ☐ **Nearly there** ☐ **Nailed it** ☐

Kapitel 8 Wörter

Hohe Zahlen / Large numbers

einundzwanzig	twenty-one (21)
zweiunddreißig	thirty-two (32)
dreiundvierzig	forty-three (43)
vierundfünfzig	fifty-four (54)
fünfundsechzig	sixty-five (65)
sechsundsiebzig	seventy-six (76)
siebenundachtzig	eighty-seven (87)
achtundneunzig	ninety-eight (98)
hundertvierundzwanzig	one hundred and twenty-four (124)
tausenddreihundert	one thousand three hundred (1,300)
zweitausendsechzehn	two thousand and sixteen (2016)
vierzigtausend	forty thousand (40,000)

Had a look ☐   Nearly there ☐   Nailed it ☐

Eine Debatte / A debate

Meiner Meinung nach …	In my opinion …
Sie sind mir wichtig, weil …	They are important to me because …
Sie sind mir nicht wichtig, weil …	They aren't important to me because …
Du hast gesagt …, aber ich denke …	You said …, but I think …
Auf der einen Seite …, aber auf der anderen Seite …	On the one hand …, but on the other hand …

Had a look ☐   Nearly there ☐   Nailed it ☐

Wo liegt das? / Where is that?

Das liegt …	It is situated …
im Norden von Asien	in the north of Asia
im Osten von Australien	in the east of Australia
im Süden von Europa	in the south of Europe
im Westen von Afrika / Amerika	in the west of Africa / America
In … spricht man …	In … they speak …
Deutsch	German
Englisch	English
Französisch	French
Italienisch	Italian
Spanisch	Spanish

Had a look ☐   Nearly there ☐   Nailed it ☐

Umwelt macht Schule / Setting environmental standards at school

Man könnte / sollte / würde …	We could / should / would …
den Müll trennen	sort the rubbish
Biomüll kompostieren	compost organic waste
eine Solaranlage installieren	install solar panels
Bienenvölker im Schulgarten halten	keep bee-hives in the school garden
Druckerpatronen / Kopierkartuschen recyceln	recycle printer / copier cartridges
Nistkästen für Vögel bauen	build bird boxes
eine Fahrradwoche organisieren	organise a bike week
Energie sparen	save energy
das Licht ausschalten	turn the light off
die Natur schützen (Naturschutz) ist wichtiger als (Müll zu trennen).	protect nature (Protecting nature) is more important than (sorting rubbish).
Der Müll ist das wichtigste Problem.	Rubbish is the most important problem.
Man sollte weniger Auto fahren.	We should drive less.
Man könnte öfter den Müll trennen.	We could sort the rubbish more often.

Had a look ☐   Nearly there ☐   Nailed it ☐

Wie werden wir „grüner"? / How do we become 'greener'?

das Aussterben von Tierarten	the extinction of animal species
die Abholzung	deforestation
die globale Erwärmung	global warming
die Lärmbelastung	noise pollution
die Luftverschmutzung	air pollution
die Überbevölkerung	over-population
die Überschwemmungen	flooding
die Wüstenbildung	desertification
… ist sehr alarmierend / gefährlich / traurig, weil …	… is very alarming / dangerous / sad because …
… ist das wichtigste / größte Problem, weil …	… is the most important / biggest problem because …
man krank werden kann	people can become ill
so viele Menschen an Hungersnot leiden	so many people suffer from starvation
sie das Leben / die Infrastruktur bedrohen	they threaten life / the infrastructure
das Ozonloch größer wird	the hole in the ozone layer gets bigger
der Planet nicht unendlich viele Menschen ernähren kann	the planet cannot feed unlimited numbers of people
wir in Zukunft diese Tiere nie mehr sehen werden	we won't see these animals any more in the future
die Wälder weniger Kohlendioxid aus der Luft absorbieren	the forests absorb less carbon dioxide from the air

K 8

43

Kapitel 8 Wörter

der saure Regen die Meere vergiftet	acid rain poisons the oceans
die Gletscher schmelzen	the glaciers melt
der Meeresspiegel steigt	the sea level rises

Had a look ☐ **Nearly there** ☐ **Nailed it** ☐

Wenn man ...	If we ...
die Luftverschmutzung reduzieren will	want to reduce air pollution
weniger Öl / Kohle / Gas nutzen will	want to use less oil / coal / gas
das Kohlendioxid in der Luft reduzieren will	want to reduce carbon dioxide in the air
keine Atomkraftwerke bauen will	don't want to build nuclear power stations
die Meere nicht vergiften will	don't want to poison the oceans
Tierarten nicht verlieren will	don't want to lose animal species
... sollte / könnte man ...	... we should / could ...
in erneuerbare Energien / Windenergie / Sonnenenergie investieren	invest in renewable energies / wind energy / solar energy
öfter mit dem Rad / öffentlichen Verkehrsmitteln fahren	travel more often by bike / public transport
weniger Ölkatastrophen verursachen	cause fewer oil spills
die Natur schützen	protect nature
Windkraftanlagen / Solarkraftwerke / Wasserkraftwerke bauen	build wind power stations / solar power stations / hydroelectric power stations
effektiver Energie und Geld sparen	save energy and money more effectively
die Wälder nicht zerstören	not destroy the forests

Had a look ☐ **Nearly there** ☐ **Nailed it** ☐

Kampagnen und gute Zwecke
Campaigns and good causes

Bali	*Bali*
Costa Rica	*Costa Rica*
die Malediven	*the Maldives*
Namibia	*Namibia*
Nepal	*Nepal*
arm	*poor*
blind	*blind*
erfolgreich	*successful*
Du könntest ... arbeiten.	*You could work ...*
ehrenamtlich / freiwillig	*voluntarily*
bei einer Tierschutzorganisation	*for an animal protection organisation*
bei einer Umweltschutzorganisation	*for an environmental organisation*
bei einer Hilfsorganisation	*for an aid organisation*
mit armen / blinden Kindern	*with poor / blind children*
mit Straßenkindern	*with street children*
mit wilden Tieren	*with wild animals*

Had a look ☐ **Nearly there** ☐ **Nailed it** ☐

Kapitel 8 Wörter

Extra words I should know for reading and listening activities

Ein sportliches Event	*A sporting event*
das Turnier(e)	tournament
die Endrunde	finals
das Halbfinale(–)	semi-final
der Sieg(e)	victory, triumph
kämpfen	to fight
das Energiegetränk(e)	energy drink
der Kleiderbeutel(–)	bag of clothes
der/die Läufer(in)	runner
das Massagebett(en)	massage bed
der/die Physiotherapeut(in)	physiotherapist
das Turnen	gymnastics

Had a look ☐ **Nearly there** ☐ **Nailed it** ☐

Festivals und Events	*Festivals and events*
aus aller Welt	from all over the world
das Drehbuch(–bücher)	(film) script
der/die Einwohner(in)	inhabitant
die Geldverschwendung(en)	waste of money
die Kapazität(en)	capacity
der/die Komponist(in)	composer
die Kritik(en)	criticism
der Künstlername(n)	pseudonym
die Modenschau(en)*	fashion show
der/die Regisseur(in)	director (film)
begrüßen	to greet, to welcome
sich qualifizieren	to qualify

Had a look ☐ **Nearly there** ☐ **Nailed it** ☐

Die Umwelt	*The environment*
der Dschungel(–)	jungle
das Erdbeben(–)	earthquake
die Naturschätze (pl)	natural resources
der Orkan(e)	hurricane
der Regenwald(–wälder)	rainforest
das Salzwasser	salt water
der Vulkan(e)	volcano
der Mangel an	lack of
drohen, bedrohen	to threaten
fehlen	to lack
retten	to save
sterben	to die
überleben	to survive
vergiften	to contaminate
verschmutzen	to pollute

Had a look ☐ **Nearly there** ☐ **Nailed it** ☐

Wie werden wir „grüner"?	*How do we become 'greener'?*
die Atomenergie	nuclear energy
der Biokraftstoff(e)*	organic fuel
die Energiesparmethode(n)	means of saving energy
der Ökostrom	'green' electricity
der Karton(s)	cardboard, cardboard box
der Verpackungsmüll	packaging waste
die Regierung(en)	government
der/die Umweltsprecher(in)	environmental spokesperson
schmutzig	dirty
verändern	to change
verbrauchen	to use, to consume (energy)

Had a look ☐ **Nearly there** ☐ **Nailed it** ☐

Kampagnen und gute Zwecke	*Campaigns and good causes*
die Armut	poverty
der faire Handel	fair trade
die Hungersnot(–nöte)	famine
das Kinderheim(e)	children's home
der Krieg(e)	war
das Menschenrecht(e)*	human right
die Tankstelle(n)	petrol station
das Trinkwasser	drinking water
die Wellblechhütte(n)	corrugated-iron hut
der Wohltätigkeitsverein(e)	charity
bedürftig	needy
unglücklich	unfortunate
sich lohnen	to be worthwhile, to be worth it

Had a look ☐ **Nearly there** ☐ **Nailed it** ☐

> ⭐ *Use your knowledge of German to work out the meaning of compound nouns. These longer words are usually made up of several smaller words, and you will often be able to work out their meaning by breaking them down and then putting the meanings back together again:
>
> die Modenschau → Mode (fashion) + Schau (show) = fashion show
>
> das Menschenrecht → Mensch (person / human) + Recht (right) = human right
>
> Sometimes you will need to take the sense of the German word and think a bit more broadly to come up with the correct English translation:
>
> der Biokraftstoff → Bio (organic) + Kraft (power) + Stoff (substance) = 'organic fuel' rather than 'organic power substance'

K8

45

ISBN 978-1-292-13241-9